ACCOUNTING

IS NOT A
FOREIGN LANGUAGE

Translating the Basics of Accounting

JEANINE PFEIFFER

Brown Books Publishing Group
Dallas, Texas

Accounting Is Not a Foreign Language
Translating the Basics of Accounting

Brown Books Publishing Group
16250 Knoll Trail Drive, Suite 205
Dallas, Texas 75248
www.BrownBooks.com
(972) 381-0009

A New Era in Publishing™

ISBN 978-1-61254-054-2
Library of Congress Control Number 2012938834

Printed in the United States of America
10 9 8 7 6 5 4 3 2 1

For more information, please visit: www.BasicAccountingTranslated.com
or www.PACAccounting.com.

To my husband, Kevin, who inspired me to write this book,
for without him, it would never have been written.

To my three children, Kiersten, Kailey, and Nicole.
You are so special to me, and I love you all dearly.

And to my father, who encouraged me every step of the way.

Contents

Acknowledgments

I had often contemplated before writing this book how I could assist people in understanding accounting; given the complexity of the field, I realized that this was no small task. My objective from the beginning of writing this book was to take out that fear and misunderstanding of a complex subject. Accomplishing that task required a year to write, compile, and edit. I would like to thank sincerely many people for their help through their guidance and dedication to my project.

David Leach, who first read my manuscript, for his assistance in leading me into the world of publishing a book and helping me begin the journey of making my book come to life.

Marla Markman, for her incredible gift of editing. I am so grateful for the time and effort you put in to edit and clarify the content.

Rayven Williams, thank you for your coordination with the many hands involved in my project, for helping make such smooth transitions, and for your patience with me in the process.

Introduction

Have you ever viewed accounting as a foreign language? Though not literally, from the standpoint of understanding it, you may feel like it is. With all those documents, numbers, journals, and ledgers, how do you make sense of everything? Like many business owners, you have likely failed to spend the requisite time to understand the process of accounting because it takes a while to clearly grasp.

Once the fear of handling their accounting takes hold, most business owners typically turn all their records over to an accountant or bookkeeper. The problem with this approach is that you will not understand what the numbers mean, which means you will not realize when you are overspending, if your customers are not paying you, or if your cash account is overdrawn—in addition to myriad other problems business owners must keep an eye on. The result of this inattention and lack of understanding is that your business is likely to fail—an outcome you surely want to avoid.

In this book, I offer an approach to accounting that will help you avoid this fate. My method will help you grasp the simplest to the most complex situations to aid you in proper accounting for your business. I start by acknowledging that accounting can seem like a foreign language to many people due to its diverse and complex format, but as I walk you through the process of making the language more understandable, you will realize it is not as difficult as it seems.

I will emphasize looking at accounting from a "foundational," "building blocks," "prep work" and "defining the most important building block" approach. This will help you start thinking about accounting in new way. As a result, you will begin to see that you can understand your accounting records and will be much more comfortable looking at your financial statements since you will know what they mean.

That is my goal: to help you understand your accounting records. Once you start down that path, you will begin to understand that it is not all about the numbers. There is so much more in between that gives a language to the numbers and in effect "transforms" them into understandable information that will help you successfully run your business.

No matter what level of schooling you have achieved, you will be able to grasp the concepts of accounting when you read this book. I will give you tips and tools to help you understand accounting in a clear, concise way. In addition, I will show you why all this will help you comprehend accounting better, and as a result, benefit your company.

It doesn't matter what industry you are in, the foundational and building block concepts of accounting are all the same. Once you learn the foundation, everything will build upon it, and other aspects of accounting will begin to make sense. Any business owner realizes that knowing that the debits equal the credits is mandatory for financial statements to be accurate. Where the uncertainty lies for most is within understanding what transactions make up the data to get to these ending balances. The goal for any business owner is to clear up that uncertainty, and I am here to help you get there.

1

The Basics of Accounting:
Interpreting the Language

Accounting is defined as the principles of practice of systematically recording, presenting, and interpreting financial accounts. It is also a statement of debits and credits. Within the accounts of debits and credits are financial transactions that relate to an asset, liability, income item, or expense. This is a rather complex definition of a word that may make it seem like a foreign language. However, it is not so complex a process that it cannot be learned.

To all of you who are skeptical about this, don't be. Sometimes it may seem a little confusing. It is all about numbers to some people, which can be overwhelming. This makes people afraid to try to understand what the numbers mean. However, I want to clear up this misconception and tell you that it is not all about the numbers—although, of course, the numbers *are* extremely important; rather it is about learning and understanding the language of accounting. To completely grasp accounting, it is imperative to know the definitions of the terms used. So that is where I will start.

It All Begins with Debits and Credits

Your first basic concept to become familiar with is the fact that accounting operates in an environment with debits and credits. A *debit* is always classified on the left side of any account; a *credit* is always classified on the right side. Furthermore, whenever any accounting transaction is entered, part of it will be entered on the debit side and part of it on the credit side. Thus, what is known as the *matching principle* is always present. In other words, all debits must match the credits, otherwise known as a double-entry system. *Double entry* means that for every debit there must be a corresponding credit.

In the realm of debits and credits, the *chart of accounts* is the first and most important step to take before you start to input any transactions into your financial records. A chart of accounts is necessary to give you a place to view all your accounts. It is a list of all your accounts in alphabetical and numerical order. Everything in accounting starts with the chart of accounts. You must have accounts to identify transactions, or you will not be able to record your data properly. For this reason, the chart of accounts must be well thought out to be a good start to understanding your financial records. You will save a lot of time, and operations will be much more efficiently financially recorded with a good chart of accounts set up. In the long run, you will benefit from seeing all accounts in an orderly manner.

Once the chart of accounts is set up, you can begin to enter data into your financial accounting system. Whether the data is entered into an accounting software application or a manual system, you need information. What information is required and where do you get it? *Source documents.* These are the original documents of data that come in the form of purchase orders, sales invoices, accounts payable invoices, loan documents, and credit card statements—just to name a few. These source documents, depending on what they are, affect sales, inventory, bill totals, cash receipts, and anything that influences the company's records. They also provide a backup in case of an audit or if a customer simply loses their copy of an invoice and requests another one. You will generate all your data from these source documents, which will lead into the debit and credit transactions.

Directing Transactions with T-Accounts

The information from the source documents will become the data that will get posted into your T-accounts. *T-accounts* are generally thought of as the way each and every account you have in your chart of accounts is set up. The *T* signifies the depiction of where the debit and credit will be put in your specific account. *Posting* is the process of entering data into its relevant place in your accounting records. Take, for example, your cash account. When you enter data from a source document—let's say a check for $500—a transaction is generated. The transaction is then put into the *T*. Let's look at it in Figure 1-1 on page below.

Figure 1-1

CASH	
(Debit Side)	(Credit Side)
	$500

In this example, you see that a check for $500 was paid to someone, so the T-account is credited for $500. If, on the other hand, your company received a check or cash from someone, the T-account will be debited for the cash received. For any transaction, your accounts will be debited or credited into these T-accounts. Your ending balance in that T-account is whatever your debits and credits net to.

Why are T-accounts so important to understand? They are where data by type of transaction is uniquely identified in your accounting records. As I mentioned earlier, you start with the chart of accounts, whereby you set up all your business operating accounts. Once the chart of accounts is set up, you enter your source document data into into your accounting records. These T-accounts are where you enter the data from your source documents.

Journals Keep It Organized

T-accounts then link into journal entries in a special way. *Journal entries* are basically a transaction that will have one or more debits and one or more credits, which are posted into a special type of journal. These journal entries are considered individual transactions that occur when you enter the information from a source document (like a T-account). The difference here is that a journal entry normally affects two or more T-accounts. Each transaction (or journal entry) will have a debit and a credit to balance. From that debit and credit, one respective T-account will be debited or credited and another T-account(s) will be debited or credited. If you were to enter a cash sale transaction into your accounting books, you would have a journal entry like Figure 1-2 on page on the following page.

Figure 1-2

	Debit	Credit
4/1/XXXX		
Cash	$500	
Sales		$500

This debit and credit will then go into T-accounts in your journals, like the cash T-account and sales T-account below (see Figures 1-3 and 1-4 below.)

Figure 1-3

CASH	
(Debit Side)	(Credit Side)
$500	

Figure 1-4

SALES	
(Debit Side)	(Credit Side)
	$500

As more journal entries are entered, more T-accounts are debited and credited. In accounting, these transactions go into special journals that are organized by type of transaction. The debits and credits inside these journals result in an ending balance, signifying a net of debits subtracted from credits or vice versa. An example of transactions for a specific account within a journal (in this case, the cash receipts journal) would look like Figure 1-5 on page below.

Figure 1-5

Cash Receipts Journal	
Debit Side	Credit Side
Invoice #2582 9/1/xxxx $1,500	Customer A Deposit 10/1/xxxx $500
Invoice #2584 10/5/xxxx $2,000	Customer B Deposit 10/15/xxxx $240
Invoice #2586 11/1/xxxx $1,000	Customer C Deposit 11/1/xxxx $800
Ending Balance: $1,960 Debit	

This account is all related to accounts receivable. If you were to look at your T-account of accounts receivable and the T-account of sales, you would see these transactions, which get posted to journals (in this instance, the cash receipts journal and sales journal), where on one side of the *T* are the debits and on the other side the credits. Within this account are dates of deposits, invoice dates, invoice numbers, and customer names. These are the details that make up the individual account. Obviously, accounts receivable also has credit transactions to account for the deposits the customers are making.

All these pieces of transactions are known as *transaction processing*, the dispensing of information into respective accounts. This is how the whole process of accounting works. Each account has debits and credits within the account, and the final balance is what the account is *netted* after the debits and credits are subtracted from one another. I am not going to expand on the details of what is in these accounts and why they are debited and credited at this time. I am only tying in the idea that all accounts can be debited and credited but nevertheless end up having either a debit or credit balance, depending on the type of account (e.g., asset, liability, owners' equity, etc.). If you become accustomed to journals, you are also becoming familiar with what people may owe you for an item you sold them or what you may owe to a vendor, for example. You will be much more effective in making sure your customers pay you on time and/or in paying vendors before late charges occur by reviewing your journals and understanding the significance the transactions inside them have on your business.

The General Ledger: The First and Last Stop

The cash receipts journal example gave you a good indication of the correlation between T-accounts and journals. All journals have transactions related to that type of journal, which in turn are defined as *cycles* in accounting. In addition to the cash receipts journal, there are four other journals in accounting. These will be discussed in greater length in chapter 5.

Many people get lost as to where all the numbers go once the source document data is entered. When the source document data gets recorded, it is processed into one of the five journals. Those transactions are then posted into something called the *general ledger*. This is where all the numbers are put in for all the transactions. Let me emphasize that you can see a trail of all the transactions from all the journals recorded into your accounting records here. A business owner must know that the transactions do go somewhere after the original source documents: first into the journals and finally to the general ledger. The general ledger, in turn, serves as a check for transactions that are going in and out of accounts, for reconciliation purposes, a backup for the company's financial records in case the data has been lost in a financial software system, and for the IRS in case of an audit. As you can see, the general ledger is incredibly important, so understanding it is essential. The only other process that occurs past the general ledger is the ending balances of the accounts that post into the financial statements (balance sheet and income statement).

To understand your accounting from the perspective of the accounts, journal entries, and posting into the general ledger, you should know that this type of processing is called transaction processing. I introduced this concept earlier in the chapter, but I want you to remember that transaction processing is a series of events that take place together—and *must* take place together—for the accounting transactions to be properly recorded.

A final process in accounting is posting. I also talked about this in various places in the chapter. What exactly is it, and why is it relevant to the accounting process? Posting is simply getting your transactions (journal entries) moved into their proper journals and financial statements (general ledger, balance sheet, and income statement). All transactions have places to go, and if they are not posted somewhere, they will not be properly recorded in your books, or your financial statements will not be accurate due to transactions that are not up-to-date.

I hope you can now picture what is involved in the process of turning numbers, documents, and data into a real accounting cycle. Looking at the basics of accounting helps define the word. Now it is not just a complex, obscure foreign language but a clear path of parts that relate to the whole. These principles lay the groundwork for the foundation I will build upon in the following chapters.

Chapter One:
What's the Point?

Accounting begins with a debit or a credit.

+ Accounting operates in an environment with debits and credits.
+ A debit is classified on the left side and a credit is classified on the right side.
+ The debits must match the number of credits; this is known as the *matching principle*.

The first step before you start to input transactions into your financial records is to set up a good chart of accounts.

+ A chart of accounts is necessary to give you a place to view all your accounts, listed alphabetically in numerical order.
+ You must have accounts to identify your transactions; otherwise you cannot record your data properly.

Source documents are necessary ingredients to shape the accounting framework.

+ Source documents provide the original documents of data information whereby you enter your data.
+ They come in many different forms, including purchase orders, sales orders, loan documents, sales invoices, and accounts payable invoices, to name a few.

You can direct transactions with your T-accounts.

+ Information from your source documents becomes the data that will get posted into your T-accounts.
+ This is the direction your transactions take in becoming a debit or credit.

+ T-accounts are important to understand simply because they are where data by type of transaction is uniquely identified in your accounting records.

Journals organize your financial information.

+ T-accounts link into journal entries in a special way. Journal entries are the transactions that will have one or more debits and one or more credits, coming from two or more T-accounts.

+ The data coming into journals posts into a special type of journal. Depending on the type of transaction, the financial data flows into that category, thus organizing the financial information into similar types.

The general ledger is the first and last stop.

+ After the original source documents, transactions are processed into one of the five journals and finally to the general ledger.

+ The general ledger is helpful as a check for the transactions going in and out, for reconciliation purposes, as a backup of financial records, and in case of a company audit.

+ Remember, *transaction processing* is a series of events that must occur together for the accounting transaction to be recorded properly.

2

Building on a Foundation:
Defining the Building Blocks of Accounting

With the basics of accounting clearly explained, you should now begin to see that accounting is not as complex as it seems. In review of the accounting basics, you should have grasped the perspective of how each important piece of accounting builds upon itself from different parts of the process. Each of the parts contributes to another (chart of accounts, source documents, T-accounts, journals, and financial statements). If you recognize this, accounting should start to become much clearer to you.

In conjunction with this idea, I am introducing a concept related to process-driven accounting for you to visualize. The concept is simple: it is a foundational and building block concept, which is taken from a basic understanding that the chart of accounts serves as the foundation of accounting. Without the chart of accounts, accounting would not exist. As a result, I call the chart of accounts the foundation, since it is unequivocally the support of the whole accounting process.

Once you have set up your chart of accounts, you can immediately start your transaction processing. This is what I call the *building process*. I will refer to the parts as the blocks. The blocks will all build up together in the processing of transactions. For example, you have an accounts payable invoice (source document). Classified as a building block, it becomes one of the blocks used to build on the foundation (chart of accounts). You also have T-accounts. These are another building block in the part of the process. T-accounts complement source documents because they are data generated from the source document. These two must be built together for the process to work. As I move to journals, understand that the T-account data generated from source documents are posted to these journals, so a supporting building block (for journals) is built. Finally, the financial statement building blocks (general ledger, balance sheet, income statement) are built on top of the other supporting data, also from a posting process. These form rows that make up a whole structure.

Working Together

You see, the sum of the parts (blocks) creates a process of transactions that flow together, yielding a whole system. However, at the same time, one block cannot work without the other.

These blocks are considered the main building blocks of accounting. This is not to say that with the foundation in place and all of the major blocks built together that the structure will stay intact. Actually, it won't. There are other blocks (which have not yet been discussed) that are required to hold the accounting cycle together. These other blocks will be covered in the next few chapters.

In Figure 2-1 (see following page), you see the illustration of the foundation and building blocks discussed in this chapter.

Obviously, by design they will not hold up without more building blocks to support them.

Figure 2-1

The Foundation and Main Building Blocks of Accounting

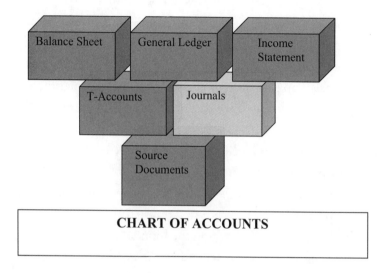

My concept of the foundation and building blocks will be part of the main theme throughout the rest of the book. Take the time to understand this now, and the rest of my discussions about accounting will fall into place.

Chapter Two:
What's the Point?

Accounting builds from different parts of a process.

+ Each of the parts contributes to one another.
+ The parts that make up the process are source documents, chart of accounts, T-accounts, journals, and financial statements.
+ Transaction processing, the dispensing of information into respective accounts, is what makes the process run.

A foundational and building blocks approach is the concept to process-driven accounting.

+ The chart of accounts serves as the foundation that supports the whole accounting process.
+ Building blocks are built on the foundation and must be built together. Data generated from one block (i.e., source documents) complements another block (T-accounts) to aid in the building process.
+ Finally, the building blocks form rows, creating a whole structure and further building the data necessary to create understandable financial information.

Transactions work together but also are a work in process.

+ The sum of the parts creates a process of transactions that flow together, yielding a whole system.
+ At the same time, one block cannot work without the other, so a work in process is also functioning at this level.
+ These blocks are considered the main building blocks of accounting. Despite the fact that these are the main building blocks (source documents, T-accounts, journals,

financial statements), their structure will not stay intact. There are other blocks required to keep the structure tightly knit.

3

The Foundation of Accounting:
The Chart of Accounts

Now that you have a grasp on the basics of accounting, let's discuss what all this data means. The chart of accounts is a good starting point since it is the foundation of our building blocks. I will begin by explaining what the different accounts are by defining their purpose, which will help you grasp how to identify what accounts you will categorize your source document financial data as. Without a chart of accounts, you cannot enter any of your source document data because you have no accounts to put them in. Once the chart of accounts is made, understanding what each account is helps you enter your data properly from the start.

Chart of Accounts Setup

The chart of accounts is pretty basic, but the larger a company is, the more complicated it can become. For most small businesses, however, the setup process is pretty simple. When you are setting up the chart of accounts, the most important thing to do first is to make sure you assign account numbers to all accounts. This will make your chart of accounts easier to read; if you have any sub-accounts, it will allow you to create those with ease once your master accounts are developed. If you do not assign numbers, you will have to put accounts at the bottom of the accounts list, which makes it difficult for you or your accountant to find what you need.

The second most important thing to do is to categorize your account numbers into sets of correlating numbers. This is important because it will allow you to add more accounts as necessary. For example, you should set up your bank accounts starting with number 1000. Your next account will be number 1010 and so on. After that, you will move on to the next type, say accounts receivable. This account should start as number 1100. To make things simpler, I've created a scenario of a chart of accounts for a typical retail store. Your chart of accounts would be set up like Figure 3-1 on the following page.

Notice that the assets are listed first. This is because the chart of accounts is always set up by this equation:

$$Assets = Liabilities + Owners' \ Equity$$

Under the main *assets* heading, *current assets* are listed first, followed by *fixed assets* and *other assets*. Following these accounts are the ones for the income statement. Starting the accounts at 1000 and increasing by increments of ten is best, as shown in Figure 3-1 on the following page. This leaves room for additions within the type of account, if needed later.

Figure 3-1

ASSETS			
Current Assets			
1000 Cash—Bank A			
1010 Cash—Bank B			
1100 Accounts Receivable			
1150 Prepaid Rent			
1200 Inventory			
Fixed Assets			
1300 Office Equipment			
1305 Office Furniture			
1310 Equipment			
1320 Accumulated Depreciation			
Other Assets			
1400 Leasehold Improvements			
1410 Goodwill			
1420 Organizational Costs			
1440 Accumulated Amortization			

Let's move on to the liabilities and equity section, where there can be a large number of accounts, depending on the company's situation. The accounts in the *liabilities* section reflect what the company owes to debtors, vendors, shareholders, and banks. As in the assets section, the accounts are separated into *current liabilities* and *long-term liabilities*. In the *equity* section, stock, working capital, owners' drawing accounts, and retained earnings are of importance. The *owners' drawing* section is of particular importance because it frequently lists many sub-accounts, as that money taken out (or drawn) to pay for medical or insurance bills must be accounted for and separated for tax purposes. This is also true of any money an owner takes out for personal funds. In Figure 3-2 below, each of these is clearly indicated.

Figure 3-2

LIABILITIES AND EQUITY
Current Liabilities
2000 Accounts Payable
2010 Inventory Purchases Receiving
2030 Payroll Payable
2040 Note Payable—Bank A
2050 Note Payable—Bank B
2060 Sales Tax Payable
2100 Mastercard—Owner A
2110 Mastercard—Owner B
2120 Visa—Owner A
2130 Visa—Owner B
2200 Customer Deposits
2300 Short-Term Loan Payable
Long-Term Liabilities
2700 Lines of Credit
2725 Line of Credit—Owner A
2750 Line of Credit—Owner B
Equity
3030 Capital Investments
3200 Owners' Drawing
3210 Contributions

LIABILITIES AND EQUITY *continued*
3220 Dental
3230 Draw
3240 Insurance—Medical
3250 Medical
3260 Prescriptions
3300 Retained Earnings

In this next section, we move into the income statement portion of the chart of accounts. What is most important in setting up this portion of the chart of accounts is that for every *sales* item, there must be a corresponding *cost of goods sold* item in which the number matches by the thousand. For example, Sales Furniture account number 4001 matches Furniture 5001 in the cost of goods sold section. This must be done in this format, since for each type of sales item (merchandise), there will be that same item's cost being cleared into cost of goods sold for each and every sale. As a result, when the financial statements are run, the percentage of markup for that item is clearly known and can be adjusted, if necessary. See Figure 3-3 below for an example of sales and cost of goods sold sections.

Figure 3-3

SALES AND COST OF GOODS SOLD
4000 Sales
4001 Furniture
4003 Paintings
4004 Lighting
4007 Accessories

SALES AND COST OF GOODS SOLD
continued
4010 Fabric
4015 Delivery (Shipping and Handling)
4045 Sales Discounts
Cost of Goods Sold
5000 Cost of Goods Sold
5001 Furniture
5003 Paintings
5004 Lighting
5007 Accessories
5010 Fabric
5015 Delivery

Finally, in the *expenses* section, the accounts are broken down by *selling, general and administrative,* and *other income and expenses.* Within the account types are categories and subcategories that represent that type of expense. This covers a large number of accounts, as you will see below. A business's chart of accounts can vary widely, but these are the most common accounts for any company. For a sample expenses section, see Figure 3-4 on the following page.

Figure 3-4

EXPENSES

Selling Expenses
6000 Commissions
6010 Advertising
6020 Freight

General and Administrative Expenses
6030 Automobile Expenses
6040 Bank Charges
6041 Bank Fees
6042 Visa Fees
6043 Line of Credit Fees
6050 Cleaning and Maintenance
6055 Computer Expenses
6060 Dues and Subscriptions
6065 Fees, Licenses, and Permits
6070 Insurance
6071 Liability Insurance
6072 Health Insurance— Employee Medical
6080 Interest Expense
6085 Internet Expense
6090 Insurance—Workers' Comp
6100 Legal
6115 Moving Costs
6120 Payroll
6121 Payroll—Owner A
6122 Payroll—Owner B
6123 Payroll—Employee A
6124 Payroll—Employee B
6125 Payroll Tax

6130 Postage and Delivery
6150 Printing and Reproduction
6160 Professional Fees
6161 Professional Fees— Accounting
6162 Professional Fees— Consulting
6163 Professional Fees— Payroll Service
6170 Rent
6180 Repairs
6181 Building Repairs
6185 Security
6190 Supplies
6192 Supplies—Office
6193 Supplies—Store
6200 Taxes
6201 Sales Tax Expense— Excise
6202 State B&O Tax
6203 Penalty—State Taxes
6204 Taxes—IRS
6210 Telephone
6220 Transportation and Gas
6230 Travel and Entertainment
6231 Car Rental
6232 Entertainment
6233 Meals
6234 Parking
6235 Telephone
6236 Travel
6240 Utilities
6241 Garbage

EXPENSES
continued

Other Income and Expenses
6300 Depreciation Expenses
6400 Other Income
6500 Other Expenses

6501 Overage and Shortage
6502 Interest Expense
6600 Prior-Period Expenses

Chart Pointers

In summary, here are some rules to keep in mind when setting up a chart of accounts:

+ Make sure the accounts are set up in the order of assets first, liabilities and owners' equity second, sales and cost of goods sold third, and finally expenses.
+ The accounts should all be in alphabetical order within the groups they are set up in.
+ Follow a guideline of spacing the accounts ten numbers apart in order to make room for additions.
+ Don't forget to add the accounts that are in multiples. For example, if there are two checking accounts, make sure both are set up separately but numbered one after the other on the chart of accounts listing.
+ If accounts have any sub-accounts, make sure to include them on the chart of accounts.

As I stated earlier, the chart of accounts is the foundation of your company's accounting system. It must be carefully set up in order to have a system that is accurate when it comes to looking at accounts in detail and supporting financial statements as well. This process should be rather simple if the chart of accounts example is followed.

Defining the Accounts

In this next section, we will take a look at each account in the order it appears in the chart of accounts and define its purpose. By learning the definitions of these accounts, you will be more certain when making decisions as to where transactions should be classified when entering data.

Balance Sheet

- *Assets, Cash:* Cash is defined as any money coming in or going out of the company's business. It is a short-term asset, meaning the account fluctuates greatly due to cash going in and out quite quickly. It can be in the form of credit cards received from customers, checks, debit cards, cash, or any other form that counts as legal money paid or received. In almost every type of transaction processing your company will do, cash is a part of it. Therefore, keeping it under a watchful eye is imperative to business success.

- *Accounts Receivable:* Your accounts receivable is a specific account that holds customers' payments on account. This account is strictly for customers who do not pay for their orders in full. Customers who pay for their orders in installments will have an account set up for them at the business that sells them the goods and will maintain running balances in accounts receivable. When customers pay for their orders in full, that's called a cash sale and it is recorded differently, as will be discussed later.

- *Prepaid Rent:* Prepaid rent (like any prepaid account) is an asset account that holds a prepayment for something— rent, in this case. The account is initially debited for the amount of the prepayment, and when the actual expense comes due, it is credited for that amount.

‧ *Inventory:* Inventory is pretty self-explanatory. It is simply anything you purchase for your business operations to sell to customers. Something to be aware of in this account is that it is a liquid asset, meaning that the account balance fluctuates greatly due to inventory going in and out quickly. Therefore, it is most typically an account that is constantly being reviewed and reconciled.

‧ *Office Equipment* : Office equipment is considered a fixed asset and must be depreciated. Some examples of office equipment are computers, fax machines, copy machines, etc.

‧ *Office Furniture:* Office furniture is also considered a fixed asset and is depreciated. Some examples of office furniture are office desks, chairs, tables, filing cabinets, etc.

‧ *Equipment:* Equipment is also considered a depreciable asset. Some examples of equipment are cell phones, routers, ten-key machines, etc.

‧ *Accumulated Depreciation:* You will find accumulated depreciation categorized under fixed assets because this is the account that will be offset by depreciation whenever any of your fixed assets are depreciated. When you look at your balance sheet and review your fixed assets, their original totals will stay the same, but the amount will be deducted by the total accumulated depreciation. This new total will tell you what your fixed assets are actually worth. This account is mandatory in any business, since all companies must report fixed assets and depreciation on those assets to the government annually.

‧ *Leasehold Improvements:* These are fixtures that are attached to the real estate (the building) you are leasing. Some examples are cabinets, light fixtures, or window treatments. Once the lease expires, the tenant can remove them as long as they don't damage the property or conflict with the lease terms. In addition, if a leasehold improvement is damaged while you are leasing the building, any repair costs associated with fixing the leasehold improvement should be classified into this account.

‹ *Goodwill:* Goodwill is considered an intangible other asset. In other words, it is not something you can touch or hold but it has value. The value of goodwill is determined by subtracting the purchases the company has from the fair market value of its assets subtracted from the purchase price of the company. The value of this asset cannot be spread over more than forty years.

‹ *Organizational Costs:* Organizational costs are any direct costs associated with starting a corporation or partnership. They can include costs to create the corporation, legal fees, accounting fees to set up the corporate books, and state incorporation fees.

‹ *Accumulated Amortization:* This account represents the gradual allocation of the cost of your intangible assets (e.g., goodwill, patents, copyrights) to expense over time. It is amortized using the straight line method and is the shorter of the asset's expected useful life or the asset's legal life.

Liabilities

‹ *Accounts Payable:* Always a current liability, accounts payable are anything you owe to creditors for something you bought for your business. This can include inventory or business expenses.

‹ *Inventory Purchases Receiving:* This is also a current liability. It is like a prepaid holding account in which your company prepays for inventory before it is delivered to you and is then reduced when inventory is received. This account is not normally used in all business operations. Manufacturing companies tend to use this account because they have large amounts of orders to be manufactured, and the cost can sometimes be too high to pay for the whole order at once. Therefore it is used to help the company keep track of orders going in and out in portions.

- *Note Payable:* A note payable is something a company gets either from a bank or an investor. It can be either short-term or long-term. Interest payments are due, as well as the principal amount of the note until paid in full.

- *Sales Tax Payable:* Any goods or items a customer buys are subject to sales tax. Your company must keep track of all the accumulated sales tax from these orders in this account. Also, when you pay business and occupation and excise taxes, you will know how much is due by looking at the balance in this account.

- *MasterCard or Visa:* These are usually credit cards a business owner possesses. You use these for business purchases.

- *Customer Deposits:* Customer deposits are made by customers for merchandise they made down payments on. They are considered liabilities, since your company still owes the merchandise to the customer until it is paid off.

- *Short-Term Loan Payable:* Any short-term loans are considered liabilities and are also something a company gets from either a bank or investor. Usually you will make interest payments toward the loan until it is paid off.

- *Line of Credit (Long-Term Note Payable):* A line of credit can also be either received by an investor or you can get one from a bank. The differences here are that it is long-term and you have more time to pay it off. Additionally, you will pay interest and payments on the principal until it is paid off.

- *Owners' Equity (Owners' Equity Accounts):* Owners' equity is classified as the owner's ownership in the business. It is an account that has a broad use. The account is used to close expenses and sales at the end of the year. It is also an account used to take draws out for purposes of distributions of cash from the business. In addition, when assets are purchased or sold, their income or losses are recorded here. Finally, stock sales, subscriptions, and purchases are also recorded in owners' equity.

- *Capital Investments:* Capital investments are anything a company invests in to provide capital for the business. It can be the business owners investing their own cash or assets into the business, or it can be equity investors who receive stock in exchange for their investment in the company.

- *Owners' Drawing:* This category is rather broad. It is mostly used to contribute cash into the business. However, it is also used for a variety of other things. When you purchase something that you put into your business with your own personal account, you can use this account to get reimbursed for it. Also, if it is necessary to draw cash for yourself out of the business, you will use owners' drawing. In addition, if you are operating your business out of your home, you can use this account to deduct a percentage of the utilities based on the size of your office.

- *Retained Earnings:* Retained earnings are the balance of sales less expenses. This account is automatically closed at year end.

Income Statement

Sales and Cost of Goods Sold

- *Sales:* Sales are a staple for bringing in money so a business can keep operating. Sales to customers are goods sold at a markup price. Whenever a customer purchases goods and takes them out of the store, sales are directly affected. A sales receipt is filled out and recorded, then the sale becomes a credit balance on the income statement and the cash is recorded as a debit. This is the typical cash-sale scenario. However, if the customer special orders merchandise, an order form is filled out instead, then once the goods reach the store or warehouse, the sale is recorded as a credit on the income statement. Timing is the critical issue in sales and it determines when the sale will be posted to the income statement (for a refresher, refer to the accounts receivable section earlier in this chapter). It's important to note that if you understand a company's sales, you can gauge its net worth.

- *Sales Returns:* Sales returns are associated with any sale that a customer decides to return to the store. When a customer returns merchandise, this account will reduce the total sale that the customer purchased. Thus net sales are a balance of sales less returns.

- *Sales Discounts:* Discounts are normally associated with accounts receivable. If customers pay off their balance early, they are entitled to a discount off the regular product price. When this happens, the entire sale will be recorded and any discounts will be deducted from the total sale amount.

- *Shipping and Delivery (Sales):* For sales, shipping and delivery charges may apply to a customer's invoice. If the customer decides to have the goods shipped to their home or business, then there will be a separate charge for shipping and delivery on their invoice. Since shipping and delivery is directly related to the sale, it will fall under the sales category, but it will be a sub-category as a type of sale.

- *Cost of Goods Sold:* This is the direct cost associated with manufacturing goods for sale. These costs could include materials used, labor to produce the product, salaries for the employees who made the items, etc. When the sale is made to a customer, a journal entry to record both cost of goods sold and sales is created so the sales price and cost of the goods is accurately reported. The sale less cost of goods sold determines gross margin—how much profit the company is making from the goods it is selling at markup.
- *Shipping and Delivery (Cost of Goods Sold):* When you receive invoices for the inventory you sell, there are shipping and delivery charges from the vendor who sold the goods to you. Therefore you must account for this separately from the actual cost of the goods. If you don't, your costs of the goods will be inaccurate due to the inclusion of vendor shipping and delivery charges. This is why this separate sub-category in the cost of goods sold account is so important to include.

Expenses

Your expenses section includes all operating expenses incurred or resources used to generate your revenue in your business. There are two types of operating expenses, selling expenses and general and administrative expenses, as shown in the chart of accounts example previously.

- *Selling Expenses:* This includes any expense associated with selling your product, such as employee commissions or freight costs.

» *Advertising Expenses:* This includes all expenses related to advertising the business, such as print ads, store signs or ads, television commercials, etc.

» *Commissions:* This is the percentage of a sale that is paid to an employee for making a sale to a customer.

» *Freight costs:* This includes any freight costs that are not part of a shipment of goods invoice. This cost is usually on a separate invoice specifically showing only freight. When an invoice with goods has freight costs on it, this should be classified as a cost of goods sold freight cost, not a selling cost.

• *General and Administrative Expenses:* This is the largest type of expense in the expenses section, since administrative expenses relate to all aspects of running your business. Following is a general explanation for each category.

» *Automobile Expenses:* If you have a vehicle that is strictly for business use, then all costs associated with the vehicle can be expensed, including vehicle maintenance, insurance, vehicle insurance, etc.

» *Bank Charges:* Bank charges should always be separated out by type of charge. This helps you determine if you are paying too many fees and in what categories the fees are mostly present. Below are the various types of fees that usually make up the bank charges section of your income statement.

  * *Bank Charge Fees:* This could include any monthly fees, overdraft charges, check-copying receipt fees, or merchant service fees.

  * *Visa Fees:* If you have a business Visa account, there can be yearly renewal fees, finance charges, and interest fees.

> * *Line of Credit Fees:* If you have a line of credit with your bank, it may charge fees for this account. This account should not be integrated with interest charges on a line of credit because these fees will be recorded in the interest expense section of the administrative expenses.
>
> * *Bank Charges–Merchant Service Fees:* When you accept credit cards from customers, you are usually charged merchant service fees.

» *Cleaning and Maintenance Expenses:* Normally, any janitorial or window cleaning service that comes to clean the building you operate falls under this expense.

» *Computer Expenses:* Examples of this expense include computer repair companies coming in to fix or set up something on your computer.

» *Dues and Subscriptions Expenses:* Dues and subscriptions can be many different things, from a subscription to a magazine to a domain site subscription for your webpage or monthly dues to host your website.

» *Fees, Licenses, and Permits Expenses:* Your tax fees, licenses, and permits fall under this category.

» *Insurance:* There are two categories here. One is for business liability insurance and the other for your employees' health insurance.

» *Interest Expenses:* Any interest on loans, lines of credit, or credit cards are shown in this category.

» *Internet Expenses:* If you prefer, you can categorize your Internet expenses here. They can also be expensed in the dues and subscriptions category. However, if you have a lot of Internet-related expenses, you may prefer this as a separate account.

» *Insurance, Employee Medical:* This category is for your employees' insurance deduction on their wages.

» *Insurance, Workers' Compensation:* Also an employee deduction expense but categorized under workers' comp.

» *Legal Expenses:* If you have any legal-related fees or charges for an attorney drawing up documents for your business, they get recorded in the legal expense category.

» *Meals and Entertainment, Owner:* Each owner (if there's more than one, of course) records their meals and the entertainment portion of their expense report in this category.

» *Moving Costs Expenses:* When your business moves to a new location, all costs associated with the move fall into this category.

» *Payroll Expenses:* These are used to report gross wages for your employees.

» *Payroll Tax:* In this category, all taxes associated with deductions from employees or employees' paychecks will be reported here.

» *Postage and Delivery Expenses:* This encompasses any postage for shipping packages or for stamps. Note, however, that delivery costs associated with goods being delivered to your warehouse or office are categorized in the cost of goods sold account, not in this category.

» *Printing and Reproduction Expenses:* Any costs related to printing brochures or advertising fliers, for example, are categorized in this account.

» *Professional Fees:* All other professional fees that are not in the other categories are listed here. Some examples of professional fees are accounting, consulting, and payroll. These fees are associated with special fees the company pays for professional services.

» *Rent, Building Repairs, Security, Supplies—Office and Store, Telephone, Utilities, and Garbage:* All these expenses are separately categorized, and all are self-explanatory.

» *Sales Taxes—Excise, State B&O Tax, and Penalty-State Taxes:* This category holds all costs associated with state sales tax expenses.

» *Taxes:* In this category you will include taxes paid to your state for sales taxes and any taxes you owe to the government.

» *Transportation and Gas Expenses:* This category holds any charges that relate to transportation, such as parking fees and gasoline.

» *Travel Expenses:* Travel expenses are strictly for business-related travel. Some examples of this category can be any meals you ate while on the business trip, lodging, car rentals, any entertainment-type activities that are business-related, or even cell phone calls and purchases as long as they correspond only to the business trip.

» *Utilities:* These are any expenses arising from power bills, garbage, recycling, etc. that help keep your business operating.

The rest of the income statement is comprised of other expenses and other income. This part of the income statement is in a separate portion since out-of-the-ordinary expenses and income are sometimes included in business operations. For example, overage and shortage expenses (for sales-tax calculation differences) and prior-period expenses (expenses related to a prior year), as well as other income not categorized as sales income, are categories that must be included in the income statement.

In upcoming chapters, I will be guiding you through each of these accounts in detail, using real business transactions and journal entries as examples. I hope the examples will further clarify the definitions of these accounts. It is imperative to know these accounts well to know how to enter your data. If you do not know how to use each account, you risk entering data into the wrong accounts, which means your records and the information they provide about your company will be inaccurate.

Chapter Three:
What's the Point?

The chart of accounts is the foundation of accounting.

+ All have a uniquely defined purpose.
+ Without the chart of accounts, you cannot enter any
  of your source document data because there will be no
  accounts to put them in.
+ Once your chart of accounts is made, understanding what
  each account is helps you identify where you should classify
  your data.

Know how to set up your chart of accounts.

+ As a small business, the chart of accounts setup is rather
  simple, although it can become more complex as the
  business grows.
+ The first step is to assign account numbers to your
  accounts, which will allow you to create your master list
  with ease. If you do not do this, you will end up placing
  accounts at the end of the accounts list. This makes it
  difficult for you and your accountant to find what you need.
+ Categorize your accounts in correlating numbers in
  numerical and alphabetical order. Leave room for
  subaccounts.
+ Always set up your chart of accounts according to this
  equation: Assets = Liabilities + Owners' Equity.
+ Leave room for your next account category by spacing them
  apart in increments of ten.
+ Assets and liabilities are separated by current and long-term.
+ In the income statement portion, remember that for
  every sales account, if you have inventory, there must be a

corresponding cost of goods sold account associated with that item.

+ Expenses are separated by type, including selling, general and administrative, and other income and expenses.

Define your accounts.

+ Defining your accounts' purpose helps you decide where to properly classify the transaction data to be entered.

+ Current assets are the most liquid accounts because the balance fluctuates, while long-term assets are subject to depreciation. As a long-term asset, the asset maintains its balance until it is sold or disposed of.

+ Other assets relate to the intangible—something you cannot touch or hold—or fixtures that are attached in some way to the building you are leasing.

+ Liabilities are classified as either current or long-term. Current include accounts payable, short-term loans, credit cards, inventory purchases receiving accounts— anything that will be paid within the year. Long-term liabilities consist of any long-term loan or note payables your company may have. These are held for over a year in duration and are subject to interest charges. These interest charges are reflected in the expenses section.

+ In the income statement, sales are goods customers buy at a markup, decreased by any costs or discounts associated with it, such as freight, delivery, or sales discounts. A corresponding cost of goods sold account is required for any company stocking inventory, which are items you purchase.

+ Operating expenses are classified by type, including selling, general and administrative, and other income and expenses.

4

The Prep Work:
Creating Understandable Financial Information

Are you learning the language yet? With the basics behind us and the foundation in place, the building blocks are in line to now be held together with support. My next topic consists of what I call the "prep work" necessary to ensure your financial information makes sense when you record your transactions. This prep work will help you define what you have been entering into your books and hold those building blocks in place.

Proper Recordkeeping Practices

The first step in getting your data ready to enter as a transaction is to know what your source documents are and to file them accurately. Although this may seem obvious, many times business owners feel like they are just too busy to file paperwork. But this task is critical because when even one source document is lost or mislaid, it creates a disorganized and chaotic business, which can result in late payments for something ordered or even lost customers. Every company has the same types of source documents that financial data should be input from. So, for any business, to understand what they represent is important. Source documents can be divided into the following seven groups:

- *Vendor paperwork:* This is considered accounts payable and includes invoices for merchandise, telephone bills, business licenses, etc.
- *Customer sales documents:* This includes cash sales or credit sales. Cash sales are considered sales receipts; credit sales are called accounts receivable.
- *Tax bills and statements:* These are considered cash-payment documents and include paperwork from the IRS, the state equalization board, sales tax and B&O, etc.
- *Business credit card statements:* If they're associated with business expenses, these are considered credit card payables.
- *Lines of credit or note payables from the bank:* These are considered short- or long-term note payables.
- *Investment paperwork from investors:* These are classified as capital investments.
- *Checks written from the company checking account:* These can be for a variety of expenses or other payments and will be the source documents for payments of any of the above accounts payable invoices. These could also be simply checks for miscellaneous charges, like a rent prepayment.

Once these source documents are grouped into their respective categories, they should be reviewed and account numbers should be written on the documents to represent where they will be entered into the accounting system. The documenting of account numbers is especially important with business credit cards. Many transactions are on credit cards and breaking them down when first receiving the statements eliminates the chances of forgetting where the transaction should be allocated to. To do this, you simply mark all the transactions on the statement with their respective expense account number. When you enter the credit card statement into your computerized system, you will put all the expenses in with their respective account numbers. You will know that you have entered all the charges when you see that the total amount of expenses data entered matches the total amount of the statement charges made. In addition, accounts receivable invoices must be grouped together by date. This will make the process of entering the customer's invoices easier, and cash receipts for the day will be accounted for accurately.

The next step in receiving and preparing the documents is of equal importance. Known as *records management,* many companies fall short in this task. By following these procedures, any company will be able to have good recordkeeping practices in place.

1. Divide accounts payable invoices to be paid by vendor name (alphabetically and chronologically) into in an accordion-type file labeled "To Be Paid."
2. Divide accounts payable invoices that have already been paid by vendor name (alphabetically and chronologically) into an accordion-type file labeled "Paid."
3. File accounts receivable invoices that are divided by date into a month-by-month file.
4. Use only checkbooks with duplicate checks and a stub to show who was paid and the amount.

Following these simple steps for the documents coming in can prevent many headaches for owners and employees alike. Just make sure the paperwork is tackled on a daily basis to keep it from piling up and becoming overwhelming.

Setting Up Policies and Procedures

Another very important step in entering your data is ensuring that you have clear and concise policies and procedures set up. All companies should have a set of policies and procedures for every job in order for the employees to do their work most effectively and efficiently. The same goes for accounting: there should be policies and procedures set up so the process of accounting can run smoothly. First, though, you must clarify what industry the company is operating in. For example, a service company does not need policies and procedures for an inventory process. Generally, however, these policies should be taken into consideration when operating any business, not only to keep the system running smoothly but also to prevent theft or misappropriation of assets.

+ Receipt of money in any form should be directed only to the person who handles the money.

+ Cash payments for customer deposits or payments should be entered by one person and money given to another person to deposit in the bank.

+ There should be only one person who handles the accounts payable invoices and writes checks for those invoices. As the business owner, you should be the only one who knows the balance of the cash account at all times and the only signer to the company checking account.

+ Inventory should be counted by workers who do not know the value of the items. Other people, normally in the accounting department, should be able to look at the values and variance totals of the inventory at hand.

+ The employee who places special orders for the customers should not be the same one who places the orders directly with the vendors.

+ The business checking account should be reconciled monthly by the bookkeeper or accountant.

These are only some of the policies and procedures that should be in place in a company. Each policy designates someone in charge but gives them segregation of duties within that department. Cash is especially important to handle in separate duties since it is so volatile and more easily hidden or embezzled by someone acting alone.

Using Memos for Supporting Blocks

For anyone to really understand how accounting works, there must be a language. Many people steer away from trying to understand accounting because it seems like a foreign language to them, as discussed at the beginning of the book. However, once you have laid the foundation, you can start putting the building blocks in place. Just like you put letters together to form words, this starts to give meaning to the data. You must be careful, however, because the blocks can fall without proper support. Memos serve as the supporting blocks to hold the main building blocks in place. Let's look at an example of how to define the journal entries in accounting using memos. A *memo* gives language to a journal entry and thus to the general ledger when posted. When a journal entry is given a memo, it's like posting a note or a key, telling others the meaning of the entry and where they can find more information about it. See Figure 4-1 below for an example of this.

Figure 4-1

10/1/XXXX	Debit	Credit
Cash	$10,000	
Cash Receipts		$10,000
Memo: Batch 500		

For this journal entry, there is a memo stating batch 500. Right away, you know that cash and cash receipts are linked into a batch of deposits. This gives the person reconciling the account at a later date a place where they can cross reference. This, in turn, gives the company a clear vision of whether they received all their cash receipts or not, as well as whether all cash receipts for the day, month, year, or however long have been recorded. Although this does not make much sense now, it will be discussed in much greater detail in the following chapters. All I want you to understand now is that the language put into the numbers (i.e., memo) makes the numbers mean something more than just totals.

Batch Memos

What does "batch" mean, and is it used only for the type of transaction shown in Figure 4-1? *Batch* usually means one or more entries of cash-receipts deposits or accounts payable invoice totals, which covers most financial transactions in a business. So, in essence, if three customers made deposits of money (cash, Visa, etc.), then the total of those deposits would be added together and placed in one batch transaction. First, this makes entering the data easier since there's only one overall total to record. Second, it eliminates the magnitude of individual cash receipts recorded onto the books. As a result, when the data on the financial statements is read, it is much more understandable and easier to reconcile since it is all put into one batch. This is the only real memo definition you would have to use in all cash receipts and checks that are paid in the company, and, as I said, it covers most of the transactions that occur in day to day operations. So, technically speaking, here is where most of the numbers are defined.

Reclass Memos

What if your company had some expenses that were not paid within the year you operated? Expenses are only kept in a business's accounting records for one year and then moved to the retained earnings account at year end. However, sometimes accounting records cannot be closed within the year. In this case, reclassification of the expenses must be done. *Reclassification* is defined as moving an expense into a prior-period expense account to clear out its total. Here's an example: if Company A had invoice #6589 from Vendor B dated 7/1/XXXX with a telephone expense of $50 on it, and it is now a year later, it must be reclassified as shown in Figure 4-2 on page below.

Figure 4-2

7/1/XXXX	Debit	Credit
Cash	$50	
Telephone Expense		$50
Memo: Reclass Vendor B Invoice #6589		
7/1/XXXX	Debit	Credit
Prior-Period Expense	$50	
Cash		$50
Memo: Reclass Vendor B Invoice #6589		

All expenses from the previous year that did not get cleared for that year can be moved into this account. This gives you a better indication of what the real expenses for the year are and what the expenses were from the previous year as an overall total.

Write-Off Memos

Sometimes, companies have customers that do not pay for a portion, or even their entire order. In these situations, normally after a year, overdue accounts are predicted to be uncollectible. How can these invoices be cleared out? The invoice becomes what is called a *write-off*. This is where the invoice is cleared, then moved into an expense account called "bad debts expense account." In Figure 4-3 below you will use the journal entries to write off a customer's accounts receivable.

Figure 4-3

12/31/XXXX	Debit	Credit
Cash	$750	
Accounts Receivable		$750
Memo: Write-off of Customer R's Invoice #25623		

12/31/XXXX	Debit	Credit
Bad Debts Expense	$750	
Cash		$750
Memo: Write-off of Customer R's Invoice #25623		

In these two general journal entries, cash was first debited and then credited to clear the write-off out of its account, since technically no money was received. Also, the accounts receivable account was credited to clear the remainder balance out of this customer's account and finally moved into the bad debts expense account. By doing this, you will be able to look at your bad debts expense account and review what customers you would prefer not to have in the future, which makes you more efficient and profitable in later years.

Adjusting Entry Memos

This type of memo is used most of the time at month end or year end when an adjustment is needed for an account relating to the wrong balance. A good example is inventory. When the inventory counts and dollar-value totals do not synch with the accounting records, an *adjusting entry* is made to correct the inventory totals so they match what is actually on hand. See Figure 4-4 below for an example of adjusting entry.

Figure 4-4

5/30/XXXX	Debit	Credit
Inventory	$2,500	
Cost of Goods Sold		$2,500
Memo: Adjustment to May Inventory for Variance		

Every one of these memos gives you an understanding of the meaning behind the numbers that are posted. A rule of thumb in using memo descriptions is to always use consistency in posting the information. If there is no consistency in using the same descriptions, over time there can be confusion as to what information is being related in the numbers. Memos give life to the numbers and create an understanding between the debits and credits they offset to provide a clear link to the represented numbers.

Pay Attention to Your Account Balances

Of utmost importance in any company is the concept of *reconciling accounts*. At a minimum, all companies are required to reconcile their bank accounts. The bank account is the most liquid and thereby requires more regular attention to its balance. Furthermore, when the bank account is not reconciled on a regular basis, the account can become overdrawn, leading to bounced checks and sometimes enormous fees. Reconciling is also done to accounts receivable, accounts payable, credit cards, and inventory. These are the other main accounts balances that are most important to keep track of.

Reconciling Checking Accounts
Let's begin with the process of reconciling your checking account. A reconcile of cash has two main distinguishable balances. One is the beginning balance; the other is the ending balance at a particular date of time, usually at the end of the month.

How does the process of reconciling get to the ending balance? First, let me back up and clarify a few things. The beginning number will always be the beginning balance number on the bank's statement. In other words, reconciling your checking account means balancing it with the bank statement numbers. Moving on, the beginning balance will be added to some numbers. These will be all the numbers that make the checking account increase. This can include deposits of cash or checks, refunds, contributions of funds into the business, etc. Simply stated, anything with cash going in represents increases of money. Second, the beginning balance will be subtracted from anything that represents cash leaving the business. This can include any checks written for expenses, merchandise payments, automatic deductions for bills, etc. With this in mind, the formula for reconciling a checking account is laid out like this:

Beginning Balance (Bank) + Deposits and Refunds −
(Less) Checks, Withdraws, and Deductions =
Ending Balance (Bank)

This ending balance will transfer over into the next month as the beginning balance of that month. What will be missing from these transactions are any deposits or refunds that have not yet cleared the bank and any checks or deductions that have not yet cleared the bank. This is because, as stated earlier, the reconciling of the bank balance is done at a particular point in time, normally at the end of a month. If any transactions have transpired since that date, the books will not match. In addition, some checks do not get cashed by their recipients within the general time frame of the month. This is why the bank's ending balance will almost never match the company's (or what's shown in the check register).

It can be determined if the company's checking account is overdrawn due to these uncleared transactions. All the uncleared transactions will still show up on the company's books, so if you net (subtract) them out from the bank's ending balance, you will have a clear indication of the "real-time balance" on that particular day. A sample bank statement is shown in Figure 4-5 below.

Figure 4-5

Bank of XXX Account Statement	
Account # 0000XXXX	
Statement Period	
1-1-XXXX to 1-31-XXXX	
Summary of Your Account	
Checking	
Business #0000XXXX	
Beginning Balance	$5,000
Deposits	$4,500
Withdraws	$1,250

Service Charges/Fees	$ 11	
Ending Balance 1/31	$ 6,739	
Business Checking Activity		
Deposits		
Posted	Transaction Description	Amount
1/01	Deposit	$1,500
1/15	Deposit	$2,000
1/25	Deposit	$1,000
Withdrawals		
Posted	Transaction Description	Amount
1/02	Purchase at Office Supply	$125
1/0	Purchase From Vendor B	$800
1/08	Withdrawal	$100
1/25	Withdrawal	$225
1/31	Service charges	$11

Notice in the bank statement that there were three deposits. The deposits listed on the bank statements are the only deposits that went through the bank. If there are others, then they will be considered uncleared. There are a number of withdrawals as well. Only the withdrawals, purchases, and checks that actually cleared the bank are on the statements. Any others will be considered uncleared and will go through subsequent bank statements.

Reconciling Credit Card Accounts

Reconciling credit cards is just as important as reconciling checking accounts. It helps you maintain awareness of the actual balance on the card and therefore not overspend or go over the card limit. Reconciling credit cards is similar to reconciling checking accounts. The only difference is that it is considered a liability account, so it is associated with purchases. A typical credit card statement shows:

$$\text{Beginning Balance} + \text{Purchases (charges)} + \text{Fees} - \text{Payments} = \text{Ending Balance}$$

Again, for reconciling purposes, the ending balance on the credit card statement will most likely not match the ending balance of the actual current balance. As a rule for understanding credit cards, the purchases will be noncurrent on the statement. All the purchases from the prior month on the statement will be selected to add to the beginning balance on the card. Fees will be added as well, and finally the payments from the last month that were made and shown on the statement will be those that are deducted from that balance. Once this process is done, the ending balance should be reconciled to the statement balance.

An important point to remember is that all transactions, whether payments, purchases, or fees, must be on the statement to reconcile the credit card. If there any outstanding payments, purchases, or fees that do not match the statement, then those amounts will be reconciled on the next statement. As long as the reconciliation was successful, these outstanding amounts will correctly show the real-time balance of the credit card.

Reconciling Accounts Receivable

Another vitally important account to reconcile is accounts receivable. It is tremendously important to keep track of accounts receivable for one significant reason: accounts receivable is the lifeblood of a business, since a business is not a business without its customers bringing in money.

To perfect a seamless accounts receivable reconciliation process, a few steps must be taken. First, though, you should understand how accounts receivable works. A customer's account originates when they buy something on account. This turns the sale into what is called *accounts receivable*. As the customer makes payments on account, cash is debited and the accounts receivable is credited. A sub-ledger entry is then automatically generated—or manually generated if a manual system is in place. This sub-ledger serves as the balancing account to the original account. For example, say Customer A bought $5,000 worth of merchandise on credit. This person pays $2,000 of the order off in one month. Another customer, Customer B, bought $6,000 worth of merchandise on credit. Customer B then pays $2,000 of that order off on the same day that month as well. The first step in reconciling this account is to make sure these two payments were batched up and deposited into one batch at the bank that day. (Batching serves as a self-check to deposits, remember?)

Also, the general ledger will list all the deposits for all customers for that day. When reconciling, the general ledger balance is checked against the customer's balance within a certain time frame. Say, for instance, that the company selling the merchandise was checking this reconciling. It should run an aged receivables report for zero to thirty days. This report will show only the balances on these customers' accounts netted by the payments they made. In addition, it should match up to the sub-ledger since that is where all deposits were cleared through. Finally, the last check can be in the checking account where the actual deposit cleared through. A company can backtrack to the actual deposits, and as mentioned previously, when they are batched up according to day and only include customer deposits, it is much easier to reconcile. If there are any discrepancies, this check will find them quickly.

In summary, accounting principles state that the balances in the accounts receivable sub-ledger should reconcile with the general ledger. As long as the deposits are batched up and deposited together, the two accounts should reconcile. So, simply stated, batching up is a simple reconciling tool for this account and our next account—accounts payable.

Reconciling Accounts Payable

Accounts payable is almost as important as accounts receivable when it comes to reconciling, due to the high-volume activity in this account. In addition, the reconciling process is almost identical to accounts receivable, except that this account is a liability account and any checks are considered payments instead of deposits.

When a company receives an accounts payable invoice, a few things happen. This invoice will be entered into a sub-ledger account for accounts payable as a credit, and the offsetting debits will go to either expenses or inventory, depending on what the invoice is for. Once the invoice begins to have payments against it, there will be a credit to the company's checking account and the reduction of accounts payable by a debit for the amount that was paid toward it. As a result, the invoice in the accounts payable sub-ledger will be reduced for this payment, and balance will be net of the payment.

A simplified way to reconcile this account is—again—to use

batches. Batching for a number of invoices will give a clear trail as to how much and what invoices were paid. When reviewing the general ledger for these transactions, there will be a debit for the invoices paid and an offsetting credit to the checking account for the payment amount. If you were to check the debit against the credit, it would equal zero since they are equal amounts posted. Again, as stated in the accounts receivable reconciling process, reconciling according to accounting principles states that the sub-ledger balances must be the same as the general ledger balances. A great way to keep these in balance is to batch your invoices through check payments, resulting in the general ledger being in balance and having a clear audit trail for communicating the payments.

Reconciling Inventory

Inventory is the type of account that is always challenging to reconcile. There are many things that can impede the accuracy of the numbers, so this account must be looked at carefully, and policies and procedures should be in place for any company detailing how the processing of inventory is handled. Reconciling procedures vary from company to company due to unique policies in place as well as different people handling the actual inventory. Most often, the companies that have inventory processing going through more hands than just one individual have bigger problems with variances.

The general guidelines listed below outline how to reconcile this volatile account. These guidelines will help you keep your inventory variances at a minimum.

+ Take the time to know the inventory, especially if it is off-site. It is important to know what the inventory is based on and the item numbers.
+ Know the high-moving items in particular since a greater

focus should always be on these goods when reconciling the account.

+ Make sure that when boxes of inventory arrive, they are checked promptly. Sometimes the wrong items are sent in the wrong boxes, which can mess up the items on hand quickly. If checked promptly, accounts payable can be notified, invoices adjusted for corrections to totals, and vendors called for returns.

+ Do not share inventory costs with the people counting the inventory. This will reduce the theft rate.

+ All staff recording sales orders for the items purchased should know well what these items are. If not, they can overlook a wrong item on an order, thus making the inventory on the books wrong.

+ Whenever merchandise is being counted, there should a baseline variance the company is willing to accept. Anything over that variance should be investigated by checking sales orders for errors and doing recounts at the company's warehouse to rule out any item miscounts.

+ If there are large variances on high-moving items, these items should be recounted more than once for accuracy.

+ Accounting staff should occasionally visit the warehouse where the inventory is received to check on how the procedures of receiving and counting of inventory are being done. This will help check for any gaps in the processes.

+ Only one person should be in charge of counting the monthly inventory. This promotes a stable count of inventory since the person knows the items well.

+ Recounts should always be done at least once after the initial count. This will determine if miscounts were done on items, or if there is actually a credible variance on the items that are off count.

For the reconciling of inventory to run smoothly, these main points should be in place in any company. There will be variances regardless of how the policies and procedures are set up due to miscounts, theft of merchandise, wrong items being received, broken items received, etc. However, there will be less of a variance on any company's inventory if good policies and procedures are in place.

Everything in Its Place

In summary, the points touched upon in this chapter are meant to clarify just how easy it can be to simplify your accounting processing. This, in effect, creates a more streamlined approach to the numbers that are recorded. We can look at this part of the process of accounting as the prep work done to hold the building blocks in place. After all, you don't just paint a wall without prepping it, do you? If you look at accounting in this perspective, you can see that there is truly more to these numbers, and doing the prepping for the work makes the job much easier in the long run. Your building blocks will stay together and give you the ability to understand your accounting records, since everything is in its rightful place.

Figure 4-6 on the next page shows our framework of accounting in building block form. Notice the foundation that supports the building blocks (the chart of accounts); next comes the building blocks of accounting, which all start from source documents and end with the general ledger, balance sheet, and income statement—the journals building block is highlighted in light grey for its special significance in understanding your accounting—and finally the prep work blocks, which support and hold the main building blocks in place.

Figure 4-6

The Foundation and Building Blocks of Accounting

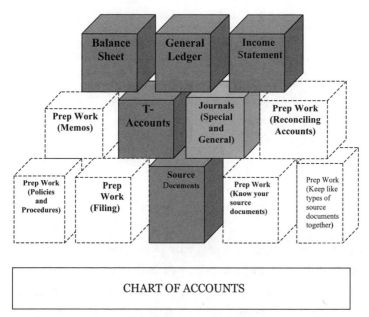

I hope you can now visualize that the building blocks in accounting are all built on the foundation. The blocks will not stay in place without the prep work being done, so doing the prep work, even though it may take you longer to do your accounting, will make your accounting records seamlessly flow together and not fall apart. Now, that we've done our prep work, in the next few chapters, we will delve more into the journals building block.

Chapter Four:
What's the Point?

The prep work blocks are the blocks that support the main building block.
+ The prep work in accounting provides all the ingredients necessary to get your financial data entered into your accounting records accurately.
+ This makes your financial information easy to read and understand.
+ It also keeps the main building blocks in place.

Maintaining proper recordkeeping practices assists in entering data properly and keeps the data in the right place.
+ Divide your source documents into seven different types: vendor paperwork, customer sales documents, tax bills and statements, business credit card statements, lines of credit or note payables from the bank, investment paperwork from investors, and checks written from the company checking account.
+ Once source documents are grouped into their respective categories, account numbers should be written on the documents to represent where they will be entered into the accounting system.
+ Records management is an important last step, defined as separating invoices and filing them in their proper places.

Policies and procedures should be set up.
+ Policies and procedures enable employees to perform their work more effectively and efficiently.

+ Remember that the industry in which your company operates determines the type of policies and procedures you should set up.

Memos serve as supporting blocks.
+ Memos are like posting a note or key describing the meaning of the entry and where information can be found about it.
+ Different types of memos help clarify financial information, aid in speeding up account reconciliation, and help track down adjustments done to accounts.
+ The types of memos most often used in accounting are batch, reclassification, write-off, and adjusting entry memos.

Pay attention to your account balances.
+ Your account balances give you a good view of the overall health of your business.
+ Reconciling accounts is crucial in maintaining accurate financial information.
+ Accounts that most commonly require reconciling are cash, accounts receivable, accounts payable, credit cards, and inventory.

5

Journey into Journals:
Understanding the Five Journals in Accounting

So far emphasis has been placed on the journals and their significance in the accounting process. Journals are substantially important in learning accounting because they are affected by every transaction you process. Thus knowing them well will give greater meaning to the language of accounting.

Part of a Cycle

In defining the journals, I must first explain the idea behind how a journal operates in the accounting environment. First, each journal is used for specific types of transactions, which are defined as *accounting cycles*. Cycles are processes of transactions that are continuously flowing. Within the cycle are all transactions that are related to that cycle. The accounts receivable, sales, inventory, and cash disbursements journals all have special cycles that flow continuously into their specific journal as data gets entered and posted.

There is only one journal that does not work as a cycle: the *general journal*. This journal picks up the rest of the transactions not included in the other four journals. Therefore the basic concept to understand is that these journals (except for the general journal) are part of a cycle. I will be showing you in the coming chapters the relevance these cycles have in learning accounting.

The five journals consist of four *special journals* and one general journal. Each is specific to the type of transaction you are recording, but as you will see later, they will eventually link together and interrelate. These journals are where most of the transactions occur in day-to-day operations.

Journal for Four, Please

Let's touch on each journal and define what is contained in them.

- *Purchases Journal, also called Inventory (special journal):* In this journal, you record any transaction that involves inventory, whether it is an invoice for receipt of inventory coming in or a customer's merchandise receipt order. In addition, if merchandise returns are generated, this is the journal that will record them.
- *Cash Receipts Journal, also called Accounts Receivable (special journal):* In this journal, you record any transaction in which a customer buys merchandise on account. If a customer pays for merchandise completed in one transaction, it would not be recorded here. This is strictly a journal for customers who have special ordered an item or bought merchandise but only paid a deposit.
- *Sales Journal (special journal):* In this journal, you record any transaction that includes a cash sale. It does not matter if the merchandise is paid for in one transaction or if it is paid for later. When the customer pays for the invoice later, it will go through the sales journal once the merchandise has been paid for in full.

- *Cash Disbursements Journal, also called Accounts Payable (special journal):* In this journal, you record any transaction that involves company purchases or bills that come for company purchases. Original source documents for things that are owed in the business generally fall into this category. Some examples are bills from a vendor for inventory you have purchased, as well as utility, tax, or rent bills, to name a few.

For Everything Else

Up until now, I have touched on the area of accounting in which transactions frequently occur. This is, in essence, the necessity of the special journals. They provide a company with an effective way to organize this frequent information chronologically, thereby enabling the business to operate much more efficiently. However, all transactions do not occur in these journals, which brings us to the questions of where these other transactions go and how they relate to the balance sheet and the income statement. I just identified the four special journals. As mentioned earlier, there is one other: the general journal is considered the main journal. For all other transactions in accounting, the general journal is used.

In the general journal, you record any transaction that involves cash, either a receipt of money (money going into the company's checking account) or money going out (money being paid out of the company's checking account). In addition, any adjustment to the financial statement accounts is done here. This is also the journal that encompasses a wide variety of special transactions, which will be discussed in a later chapter. However, as I explained earlier, cycles are not a part of how this journal operates.

Following are the types of transactions that get recorded in the general journal:

- *Any prepaids:* These are anything for which a company has paid in advance, such as rent, merchandise, etc. The originating entry will debit the prepaid (liability) account and credit cash.
- *Customer deposits for credit sales:* These are customer deposits for merchandise orders. The original entry will debit the customer deposits (liability) account and credit cash.
- *Payroll expenses:* The original entry will debit the salaries payable (liability) account along with payroll tax expenses and credit cash.
- *Owners' draws:* This is for any cash you take out of the business to pay yourself outside of payroll or for any personal purchases. The original entry will debit the owners' drawing (equity account) and credit cash.
- *Depreciation expense:* The assets your company owns must be depreciated monthly for tax purposes, so an adjusting entry to reduce the balance is required. The original entry will debit depreciation expenses and credit accumulated depreciation (a contra-asset account, meaning an account that offsets asset accounts to show their remaining value after depreciation deductions).
- *Miscellaneous charges:* This covers anything that arises in which you have to pay for something with a check or cash, such as a freight charge when a vendor delivers merchandise to your company. The original entry will debit freight expenses and credit cash.

All these examples affect either the balance sheet or the income statement. The liabilities, accumulated depreciation, and equity affect the balance sheet, and the expenses affect the income statement. One other important point to note is that since cash transactions are always recorded in the general journal, it's a good place to see where you are spending your money and observe spending patterns in your business.

When you know your chart of accounts (the accounts where your data will be recorded), you can begin to put this information into its unique journal. Once the data is its rightful place, the journals hold all this vital information securely through each continuous accounting cycle.

Chapter Five:
What's the Point?

The journals are part of a cycle.

+ Journals are substantially important in learning accounting because they are affected by every transaction you process.
+ Each journal is used for specific types of transactions, which are defined as the *accounting cycles.*
+ Within the cycle are transactions that are related to that cycle.
+ Only one journal does not work as a cycle—the *general journal.* The general journal picks up all the other transactions not included in the other four journals.
+ The five journals consist of four special journals and one other journal, the *general journal.*

There are four special journals.

‹ *Purchases journal (inventory journal):* Here is where you record all inventory transactions.
‹ *Cash receipts journal (accounts receivable):* This is where you record transactions when customers buy merchandise on account.
‹ *Sales journal (sales book):* Here is where you record cash sales. It does not matter if the merchandise is paid for in one transaction or later on—it will go through the sales journal once the invoice has been paid in full.
‹ *Cash disbursements journal (accounts payable journal):* This is the journal where you record any transaction that involves company purchases or bills that come for company expenses.

The rest of the transactions that do not belong in the four special journals get recorded in the general journal.

+ In the general journal you record any transaction that involves cash, either a receipt of money or money going out. In addition, any adjustment to the financial statement accounts is done here.

+ Different types of transactions are classified as either prepaids, customer deposits for credit sales, payroll expenses, owners' draws, depreciation expenses, or other miscellaneous charges.

6

Your Key to Accounting:
Learning the LINKS Approach

We have spent a considerable amount of time discussing the foundational aspects of accounting, building upon that foundation with the building blocks necessary for the process of accounting to happen correctly, and doing the prep work to keep the building blocks together. In addition, we have devoted a chapter entirely to understanding the journals in accounting, explaining that they serve a valuable purpose in the accounting cycle. All these perspectives are vital to clearly grasp the concept of how accounting actually works.

We are now going to take the next step and show how the journal building block (the one highlighted in light grey in Figure 4-6 on page 59) is one of the most essential building blocks to understand. You will understand almost everything there is to know to do your own accounting if you can completely understand the significance of the journals—more specifically the approach I am about to discuss. It is called the L-I-N-K-S approach.

Connected Together

Let's start by reviewing that there are five journals in the journals building block: the main journal (general journal) and the four special journals (purchases, cash disbursements, cash receipts, and sales journals). Each journal contains detailed information in journal entries that were originally entered from source documents, then debits and credits posted to their respective T-accounts. This data goes into the respective journals from the T-accounts.

Figure 6-1

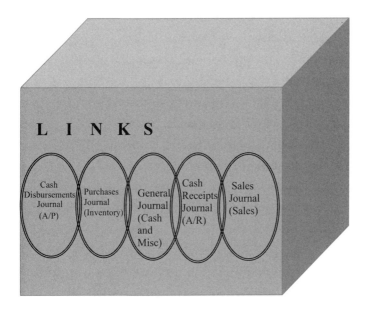

The journals in Figure 6-1 (on previous page) are held together and named LINKS—short for linkage or connection. This concept is important to understand because this connection holds the most vital transactions your business will encounter in everyday business operations. In the LINKS chart, each of the letters stands for a part of accounting and is designated as a special or general journal:

+ Liabilities owed (cash disbursements journal)
+ Inventory reserved (purchases journal)
+ Necessary other journal entries (general journal)
+ Keeping cash receipts recorded (cash receipts journal)
+ Sales held here (sales journal)

In addition to the construction in Figure 6-1, there are other combinations of the LINKS connections. The inventory cycle, for example, uses all five links; the cash receipts cycle uses three or five links; as does the accounts payable cycle. Also, one of the links actually operates apart from the others, and in some situations, it acts outside the other accounting cycles. This disconnected link is still included but is not involved in the way the cycles operate. We will be discussing this disconnected link in an upcoming chapter.

Cycles play a crucial role in keeping the LINKS connected. Each part of the process that occurs when a cycle is operating requires all the links in that cycle to stay together. If they do not, the cycle will not operate continually and thus your accounting data will be inaccurately recorded. Therefore, as a result of following the connected links, by design your cycles will operate as a true accounting cycle.

The Next Step

The LINKS concept builds within the journals previously defined in the last chapter. I originally explained that when you begin to know the journals, you will start to comprehend how the process of accounting really works. Taking it a step further by defining this in a broader sense, within these journals are debits and credits. The debits and credits spread out into their respective journals as different types of cycles operate. Becoming familiar with the different combinations of linkages helps you understand the various cycles and what accounts and types of transactions are included in them, since they require special and general journals linked together for the cycle to flow.

In simple terms, the connections represent the journal-entry recording process, from the data making its way into two or more special (or general) journals, to posting to the general ledger, and finally to the financial statements (balance sheet and income statement). It is the whole accounting cycle. Remember, the definition of accounting is the principles of practice of systematically recording (from source documents to the T-accounts and into journals), presenting, and interpreting financial accounts. It is also a statement of debits and credits (general ledger, balance sheet, and income statement ending balances). Within the accounts of debits and credits are financial transactions that relate to an asset, liability, income item, or expense (the LINKS).

In the LINKS chart, I have inserted in parentheses the parts of accounting that have been discussed so far. By reviewing the definitions, you should see how the connection forms the accounting process by following the steps discussed in the previous chapters—most importantly, the LINKS approach. As the linkage connects, the accounting cycle operates, following a specific path of processing and recording the transactions.

In summary, understanding these LINKS in detail and the transactions that flow through them will prepare your mind to look at accounting in a different way. In upcoming chapters, I will be discussing specific accounting cycles in more detail, highlighting the importance of the LINKS approach in the accounting cycle involved.

Chapter Six:
What's the Point?

Journals are a building block, a significant piece in helping you understand accounting.

+ The journals building block is one of the most essential building blocks to understand.

+ You will understand almost everything there is to know to do your own accounting if you can understand the significance of the journals.

It is important to understand how the LINKS are connected together.

+ The LINKS (or linkage) connect all the parts of accounting together.

+ Each part of the link stands for a part of accounting and is designated as a special or general journal.

  » *L* is for liabilities owed (cash disbursements journal).

  » *I* is for inventory reserved (purchases journal).

  » *N* is for necessary other journal entries (general journal).

  » *K* is for keeping cash receipts recorded (cash receipts journal).

  » *S* is for sales held here (sales journal).

+ Different LINKS combinations are used for different cycles. For example, inventory uses five links, accounts receivable uses three or five links, and the accounts payable cycle uses three links.

7

Stock Answers:
Using the Inventory Cycle in the LINKS Approach

In this chapter, I will be discussing inventory as one of the main accounts that generate most of your transaction processing in your accounting cycle. Of course, not all companies have inventory. Furthermore, when inventory is what is sold to customers to make a sale, the inventory cycle is relevant, but if the company does not have inventory, this cycle is not relevant and therefore not required. For our purposes in this chapter, I will be showing you how to process transactions if your company does have inventory, focusing most of my attention on situations where inventory is involved in any transaction processing event. As a result, I will also be using examples with other interconnected cycles, such as accounts receivable. Although accounts receivable is an important part of the inventory cycle, it is not the focal point, so this chapter will still primarily focus on the topic at hand. In chapter 8, I will get into the cash receipts cycle, including more detailed topics on customers and special situations regarding cash receipts.

For now, let us begin by talking about the inventory cycle. The inventory account is quite complex; however, with knowledge and understanding, anyone can handle the challenge of keeping inventory well maintained through their books. Let's start with a basic definition of the inventory cycle: a process of purchasing and receiving goods, creating orders for customers for the goods reserved or available, shipping and delivering those goods to the customer, and keeping track of all the goods coming in and going out of stock. Outside this basic definition, if you want to grasp the full concept of inventory, we also need to relate it to the other accounts in the LINKS diagram, since they are all part of the inventory cycle. (Remember from the previous chapter that LINKS stands for liabilities owed for inventory, inventory reserved for customers, necessary journal entries, keeping cash receipts records, and sales held in.)

The Inventory Process

How is inventory created on your books in the first place? To start with, there must always be a purchase order. *A purchase order* is a product request for a *vendor* (a company you buy goods from) that lists the specific items wanted in the quantities desired.

Note how I mentioned the word "order." This simple word will be repeated a number of times in talking about inventory. An order is *always* nonposting, although it does have dollar amounts and totals on it. In other words, nothing is going to post onto the general ledger with any dollar amounts until something reaches the invoice stage. That being said, let's move on with the process.

When you or whoever is ordering the merchandise is comfortable with the items and quantities of those items on the purchase order, you will call the vendor and place the order. Once this is done, the company who placed the purchase order will receive what is called an *acknowledgment* from the vendor. At this point, the person ordering must review this acknowledgment paperwork carefully, because it is considered a formal agreement that the goods have been ordered at the quantities and price requested. If the amount ordered or the prices are wrong, the person ordering the goods still has the ability to change what the vendor acknowledged. So often this step in the inventory process is overlooked, and companies pay more for the goods than they should or sometimes do not realize that the quantities on the purchase order do not match what is on the acknowledgment. This mistake will not get caught if it does not go through the acknowledgement process. Likewise, *inventory variances* (differences in actual inventory on hand and what is shown on stock on a company's computer report) will occur.

Sometimes customers will be the ones ordering these goods through your company. In those cases, you will need to write up a *sales order*. The sales order will show items on it with quantities ordered, cost, and price of the goods. Since it is only an order, it has not reached posting status, so no amounts are posted to the general ledger. This should make sense, since the items have not even been delivered to the company that has placed the order for these items.

Once the items arrive, the paperwork again becomes vitally important to make sure all goods that were ordered were received and at the correct prices. Two documents come with the order; one is the packing list. Sometimes there are prices on the packing list but not always. However, the quantities of the goods ordered are always listed, so it is a good self-check to review this. You will check this against the acknowledgment for quantities ordered as well as prices of merchandise on the order. Second, there should now be an invoice (also called an *A/P invoice*), which will list items with full costs and totals. Looking at the accounts payable (A/P) invoice in Figure 7-1 (below), you will see the purchase order number (P/O) is referenced on it, as is an acknowledgment number that is associated with the order. In addition, cost and quantities of goods are shown on the invoice along with the *extension* (total cost).

Vendor C				
Date 5/10/XXXX				
Invoice #865491				
R/E: P/O #200				
Acknowledgment #956257				
Item	Description	Cost	Quantity	Cost Extension
#W235	Armchair Vendor Y	$1,000	5	$5,000
#W236	Sofa Vendor X	$15,000	1	$15,000
Total Invoice				$20,000

Remember how I said that orders were nonposting? Now that an invoice has been received, the goods can be entered into the company's computer inventory system to be finally recognized as actual inventory with a total price. Also, if all the items on the purchase order have been received, this purchase order is now closed. However, if there are outstanding items, the purchase order will not be closed until the full quantities have been received.

Two things happen when the invoice is received. First, the accounts payable invoice will be read and proper quantities will be listed in the computer inventory system. What this does is fill the back orders for the customers who ordered that item. Second, the sales order (S/O) that was placed by the customer can be closed and a sales invoice can be created with the total costs of the items listed. Figure 7-2 (below) shows the journal entries that occur when the invoicing happens.

Figure 7-2

Journal Entry 1		
5/15/XXXX	**Debit**	**Credit**
Inventory	$5,000	
Accounts Payable		$5,000
Memo: Invoice #865491		
Journal Entry 2		
5/15/XXXX	**Debit**	**Credit**
Cost of Goods Sold	$1,000	
Inventory		$1,000
Memo: S/O #W5500		
Journal Entry 3		
5/15/XXXX	**Debit**	**Credit**
Accounts Receivable	$1,500	
Sales		$1,500
Memo: Customer T Invoice #6000		

As noted, the inventory went into stock, thereby increasing the balance in the inventory and accounts payable accounts (journal entry 1). Second, the cost of goods sold is increased and inventory then decreased for the sales order #W5500 that was received (journal entry 2). In addition, the sales and corresponding accounts receivable accounts are charged for the same customer, Customer T, since his merchandise has been received (journal entry 3). The totals reflect a markup price, since companies do not sell their goods at cost.

So there you have it: This is the full process of an item becoming inventory. In summary, it starts as P/O (purchase order) and S/O (sales order), then moves to A/P (accounts payable), where the invoice gets put into inventory at cost, and finally the sales invoice is prepared with items charged at a markup price.

Other times the items that a customer wants are already in stock at the store or warehouse that holds the merchandise. How is the process different than when a customer orders an item that is out of stock? Simply put, the difference is that when the item is in stock, the order will automatically go from a sales order directly to the invoice stage. At this point, the inventory is also automatically reserved for this customer on the order and flows into the sales invoice, where the customer gets billed. Stock will then decrease for the item that this customer ordered, and the sale is recorded in respective journals via entries similar to the ones in journal entries 1 and 2.

When You Have to Prepay for Goods

Inventory is not always as straightforward as the process above. For instance, some companies have to prepay for their goods even before they have been made. In this situation, an accounts payable invoice will not come into play until the goods have been prepaid for. Normally, as mentioned above, all transactions are nonposting until the inventory arrives. However, when companies must purchase the goods by prepaying for them, there is a simplified accounting method to do this. The company sets up a special account on the balance sheet titled "Inventory Purchases Receiving." This is like a "holding account" to prepay for the goods until the items are received. Let's look at a typical transaction: Say Company A needs to purchase fifty boats for their showroom, which costs $100,000. The vendor requires the company to prepay for the boats before they even start making them. As a result, they will prepay with a check to get the process started. There will be a purchase order generated for the items and quantities needed. Figure 7-3 below shows the journal entry:

Figure 7-3

6/1/XXXX	Debit	Credit
Inventory Purchases Receiving	$100,000	
Cash		$100,000
Memo: Wire Transfer to Vendor M		

Once the vendor receives the money, it will start the manufacturing process to make the products Company A is buying. The vendor may not actually make all the goods Company A is requesting, so good accounting is necessary. Say the vendor sends Company A twenty-five of the fifty boats from purchase order 25. Figure 7-4 on the following page shows the corresponding journal entry.

Figure 7-4

7/1/XXXX	Debit	Credit
Inventory	$50,000	
Inventory Purchases Receiving		$50,000
Memo: Receipt of Vendor M Invoice #23565 on P/O #25		

From this entry, accounts payable will create an invoice for the amounts on the order, and the corresponding purchase order will be closed for the items and quantities on the order. An invoice for the corresponding journal entry is then created.

Controlling Inventory Variances

No matter what inventory method a company uses, there are bound to be *inventory variances*. Variances occur when the inventory that has been counted at the warehouse does not match the amount of inventory showing in your accounting records. When this situation occurs, it will be necessary to do recounts on the products that are showing variances. Once this is done, further recounts can be also done on the highest variance items. This is necessary since these items affect your company's bottom line totals so heavily. However, no matter how you slice it, there is most likely always going to be a variance on some items. How, then, can you account for these variances to get the books to match the actual counts on hand? Figure 7-5 on the following page shows a typical example of accounting for an item that showed up as one additional item in the warehouse, which conflicted with the accounting records showing one less than the warehouse. Each Item #W344 costs $325, so for this example, one of item #W344 is added to the books at the item's cost.

Figure 7-5

6/30/XXXX	Debit	Credit
Inventory (Item #W344)	$325	
Cost of Goods Sold (Item #W344)		$325
Memo: COGS Adjustment for Item #W344 to 6/30 Inventory Count		

Notice on the journal entry that the inventory account was debited (increased) for the item that was not showing up on the books accurately. The cost of goods sold account is then credited for the cost of the item in its cost of goods sold account. This journal entry could be reversed to account for the opposite transaction, for when the warehouse count finds less than originally counted.

How LINKS Works in the Inventory Cycle

Let's get back to how we started this chapter: How does the LINKS approach work in the inventory cycle? In the charts that follow (Figure 7-6 on the following pages), you will see how each link connects, and within those links are debits and credits, following the matching principal of accounting. You will also see the journals (which originate from T-accounts), shown here with the LINKS letters associated with them, and the posting from the special/general journals into the general ledger, as well as the balance sheet and income statement.

Figure 7-6

A/P Journal or Cash Disbursements Journal=L	
Debit	**Credit**
A/P MC Batch 500 10/1/ XXXX $5,000	Inv #23575 12/31/XXXX $12,5000
A/P MC Batch 501 12/31/ XXXX $5,000	Inv #R87495 12/31/XXXX $10,000
A/P MC Batch 502 12/31/ XXXX $8,000	

Purchases Journal=I	
Debit	**Credit**
Inv #W23575 12/31/XXXX $12,500	S/O batch 989 12/31/XXXX $500
Inv #R78495 12/31/XXXX $10,000	S/O batch 990 12/31/XXXX $600

General Journal=N	
Debit	**Credit**
Batch 250 10/1/XXXX $2,500	A/P MC Batch 500 11/1/ XXXX $5,000
Batch 251 11/1/XXXX $1,000	A/P MC Batch 501 12/31/ XXXX $5,000
	A/P MC Batch 502 12/31/ XXXX $8,000

Cash Receipts Journal=K	
Debit	**Credit**
Inv #2582 10/1/XXXX $1,500	Batch 250 11/1/XXXX $2,500
Inv #2584 11/1/XXXX $2,000	Batch 251 11/1/XXXX $1,500
Inv #2585 11/1/XXXX $2,000	A/P MC Batch 502 12/31/ XXXX $8,000

Sales Journal=S	
Debit	**Credit**
Discount Inv #2582 11/1/ XXXX $30	Inv #2582 10/1/XXXX $1,500

The transactions from the original journal entries into the books, shown in Figure 7-6, are automatically put through the general ledger. Each journal in the inventory cycle is linked into the general ledger and flows into a scheme of numbers with debits and credits and ending balances. Figure 7-7 (see pages 88–89) is a depiction of how the general ledger would look from posting all these transactions into it.

As you see, there is a *split* column. This column is the account that you will debit or credit when you are entering the journal entry. Remember in chapter 1 where I discussed double-entry accounting? There must be a debit and a credit for each transaction. The general ledger references the other side of your transaction through this "split."

Figure 7-7

General Ledger

Company XYZ

For period 10/10/XXXX–12/31/XXXX

1002 Cash

Type	Date	Name	Memo	Split	Debit	Credit	Balance
							$25,000
Check	10/1/ XXXX	Deposit	Batch 250	Accounts Receivable	$2,500		$27,500
Check	11/1/ XXXX	Deposit	Batch 251	Accounts Receivable	$1,000		$28,500
Payment	11/1/ XXXX	Manual Check	Batch 500	Accounts Receivable		$5,000	$23,500
Payment	12/31/ XXXX	Manual Check	Batch 501	Accounts Receivable		$5,000	$18,500
Payment	12/31/ XXXX	Manual Check	Batch 502	Accounts Receivable		$8,000	$10,500
				Ending Balance:			$10,500

1400 Accounts Receivable

Type	Date	Name	Memo	Split	Debit	Credit	Balance
							$5,000
Invoice	10/1/ XXXX	Customer A	Inv #2582	Sales	$1,500		$6,500
Invoice	11/1/ XXXX	Customer B	Inv #2584	Sales	$2,000		$8,500
Invoice	11/1/ XXXX	Customer C	Inv #2585	Sales	$2,500		$11,000
Payment	11/1/ XXXX	Customer C	Batch 250	Cash		$2,500	$8,500
Payment	11/1/ XXXX	Customer A	Batch 251	Cash		$1,500	$7,500
				Ending Balance:			$7,500

2000 Accounts Payable

Type	Date	Name	Memo	Split	Debit	Credit	Balance
							$25,000
Payment	10/1/ XXXX	Manual Checks	Batch 500	Cash	$5,000		$20,000
Payment	12/31/ XXXX	Manual Checks	Batch 501	Cash	$5,000		$15,000
Payment	12/31/ XXXX	Manual Checks	Batch 502	Cash	$8,000		$7,000
Invoice	12/31/ XXXX	Inv #23575, #23576	Batch All	Inventory		$12,500	$20,000
Invoice	12/31/ XXXX	Inv #R78495, #R78946	Batch All	Inventory		$10,000	$29,500
				Ending Balance:			$29,500

1500 Inventory

Type	Date	Name	Memo	Split	Debit	Credit	Balance
							$20,000
Invoice	12/31/ XXXX	Inv #23575		A/P	$12,500		$32,500
Invoice	12/31/ XXXX	Inv #R78495		A/P	$10,000		$42,500
Sales Order	12/31/ XXXX		Batch 989	Costs of Goods Sold		$500	$43,000
Sales Order	12/31/ XXXX		Batch 990	Costs of Goods Sold		$600	$43,600
				Ending Balance:			$43,600

5000 Sales

Type	Date	Name	Memo	Split	Debit	Credit	Balance
							$25,000
Invoice	10/1/ XXXX	Customer A	Inv #2582	Sales		$1,500	$26,500
Invoice	11/1/ XXXX	Customer B	Inv #2584	Sales		$2,000	$28,500
Invoice	11/1/ XXXX	Customer C	Inv #2585	Sales		$2,500	$31,000
Discount	11/1/ XXXX	Customer B	Inv #2584	Sales Discount	$30		$30,970
				Ending Balance:			$30,970

5050 Sales Discounts

Type	Date	Name	Memo	Split	Debit	Credit	Balance
							$500
Discount	11/1/ XXXX	Customer B	Inv #2584	Sales		$30	$530
				Ending Balance:			$530

The final two building blocks in our inventory cycle are the balance sheet and the income statement. Let's look at the balance sheet first (see Figure 7-8 on the following page). Simply stated, the balance sheet is a financial statement showing the general ledger ending balances of all assets, liabilities, and owners' equity accounts from the LINKS figure.

Figure 7-8

Balance Sheet	
Company XYZ	
For the year ended 12/31/XXXX	
Balance	
Assets	
Current Assets	
Cash	$10,500
Account Receivable	$7,500
Inventory	$43,600
Total Assets	$61,600
Liabilities and Owners Equity	
Accounts Payable	$29,500
Owners Equity	$32,100
Total Liabilities + Owners Equity	$61,600

The income statement in Figure 7-9 (on the following page) shows sales, cost of goods sold, and sales discounts. It shows all the operating expenses you have. In other words, your income statement is technically all of the costs associated with running your business. Looking at it from the perspective of the LINKS figure, these entries result from the sales journal and purchases portion of the diagram as well as from the ending balances of the general ledger. You should now clearly see that there is a definite interrelation between all these accounts to the journals, general ledger, balance sheet, and income statement, which makes the process of accounting work properly.

Figure 7-9

Income Statement	
Company XYZ	
For Period 10/1/XXXX – 12/31/XXXX	
Sales	
10/1/XXXX Invoice #2582	$1,000
11/1/XXXX Invoice #2584	$2,000
12/1/XXXX Invoice #2585	$2,500
Gross Sales	$5,500
Less Sales Discounts	
12/1/XXXX Invoice #2584	$(30.00)
Net Sales	$5,470
Cost of Goods Sold	
Item W	$500
Item X	$600
Net Income	$4,370

As you can see, inventory is rather complicated. However, if the inventory cycle is followed using the LINKS approach, with policies and procedures in place, it will prevent you from having high variances on the items you sell. Your inventory will also be organized, well counted, with few or minor errors, and you will not have to recount your inventory very often. This will lead to greater profits for your company and more cash on hand, creating a stable environment for your company to prosper.

Chapter Seven:
What's the Point?

Inventory must follow a process.

- To start with, there must always be a *purchase order*, a product request for a *vendor* that lists the specific items wanted in the quantities desired.

- An *order* is always nonposting.

- Once the order is placed, an *acknowledgement* is received from the *vendor*. The acknowledgment serves as a formal agreement that the goods have been ordered in the quantities and prices requested.

- Sometimes customers order goods through your company. In this case, a *sales order* is written up. This order is still nonposting since it is only an order. It will list only quantities, cost, and price of goods and does not go through the general ledger yet.

- Once the order arrives, the *acknowledgement* is compared with what is called a *packing list*. Sometimes there is no *packing list*, but when there is, the packing list shows all items shipped with quantities and cost extensions of the items ordered.

- An *accounts payable invoice* comes with the acknowledgment and supporting packing list, which shows items with full costs and totals. Now that the goods are invoiced and received, it is time to post them into the computer inventory system.

This process affects inventory, cost of goods sold, accounts payable, accounts receivable, and sales—all of the LINKS.

+ The process changes when you have to prepay for goods.
+ In the event that your company must prepay for goods before they are made, you must account for the prepayments in a different way since the goods are not yet considered inventory.
+ An account called *inventory purchases receiving* is set up in these types of situations. It is like a "holding account" to prepay for the goods until they arrive at your warehouse.
+ Only inventory purchases receiving and your cash account are affected by this type of transaction.
+ Once the goods are received, an *accounts payable* invoice will come for the items prepaid for, and the corresponding *purchase order* will be closed for the items and quantities on the order.

You can control inventory variances.

+ Variances occur when the inventory that has been counted at your warehouse does not match the amount of inventory showing on your accounting records.
+ Accounting for the variances requires an adjustment to your inventory and cost of goods sold accounts.

8

Money Matters:
Using the Cash Receipts Cycle in the LINKS Approach

In the last few chapters I have given you the methods to help you better understand your financial information, but most importantly you have been given the foundational building blocks and prep work involved to show you that accounting is a step-by-step process. Within the journals step, the LINKS approach is most notably the key to understanding the language of accounting. I started explaining to you in chapter 6 how all the LINKS are associated together in the inventory cycle, the most important transaction processing cycle to understand. Let me reiterate that what is in each of these links will be most of the knowledge you will need to understand accounting and successfully do it by yourself. Moreover, recall that the accounts inside each LINKS journal are where the bulk of your everyday business transactions originate. Furthermore, the LINKS form a chain in the transaction processes that must not break apart. If any of the links do fall apart, then the transaction process will not be recording accurate information. Understanding the LINKS in a transaction process is essential for you to know the language of accounting. In this chapter, I will focus on these individual accounts and illustrate to you how different types of transactions occur. Detailed information on individual accounts that make up these LINKS will be provided, all of which are a part of the chart of accounts. This directs you to the further connection of the foundation of accounting (chart of accounts) and how it ties in to other aspects that are built up from it.

What Are We Looking At?

Let's begin this chapter with a discussion of accounts receivable and sales. These accounts are part of the cash receipts journal and sales journal LINK. They are two of the highest transaction generating accounts in the LINKS system (other than inventory) that together make up all of a customer's order data. In the processing of accounts receivable, all the LINKS come into play. For the cash receipts cycle, there are two different versions of the LINKS approach: With inventory, all the LINKS are used. Without inventory, only the NKS links are used.

To understand this in simple terms, just remember that the transaction processing that is occurring here is all related to customers (of all different names) purchasing goods. These are all the accounts that are affected when cash receipts and sales transactions are generated in any business. The cash receipts cycle is a transaction process that records a sale from the purchase through receipt of goods and payment. The accounts balances are reduced at a rapid rate, and only certain transactions related to this cycle are included in the transaction processing. I will describe all these accounts in this chapter.

Special Order Sales

As a business owner, you want potential customers to be able to purchase your inventory in as many different ways as possible in order to attract more business. To have a successful business and satisfied customers, you must understand the accounting behind these various ways to sell merchandise.

Let's take a look at special orders, which just one way of selling merchandise to your customers. How is this handled in accounting transaction processing? To start with, understand that when the customer is purchasing something that is not actually in stock at the store, it must be recorded as a credit sale—in other words, accounts receivable. Naturally, every business has some amount of accounts receivable on their books on a weekly or monthly basis. While it is favorable to have many customers, keeping track of what they owe can become tedious and time consuming unless you can understand how to account for the transactions. To completely understand the transaction process that occurs for a special order, it is imperative to show the breakdown of paperwork used, the transaction entries, and the final entry to complete the process accurately.

Before we discuss accounting for special orders, there is another concept I must bring to your attention in regard to the cash receipts cycle. It is the concept of understanding accounts receivable in the terms of accrual accounting. *Accrual accounting* is defined as a method of accounting recognized expenses when incurred and revenues when earned regardless of when the cash is received. In other words, for accrual accounting to be in place, an accounts receivable invoice sale will only be recorded when the sale is complete. The sale will stay "pending"—not recorded on the books—until the sale has shipped out to the customer. Normally, once all cash is received for a customer's order, a company will ship out the merchandise, thus an actual sale is recorded at this time. As a result, accounts receivable will be credited and sales debited for the entire sale. The sale will then go through the general ledger and will be present on the income statement as well.

This process of accounting is a crucial element of recording a special order correctly. I am touching on the concept of accrual accounting in this portion of the book primarily due to the nature of accounts receivable. Accounts receivable is the main account involved in the accrual type of accounting. The other type of accounting is cash, which recognizes a sale when cash is received. You may choose which type of method you want to use; however, the accrual method is more widely used. By nature, cash receipts fall into this category of cash versus accrual by simply being an account into which money is placed.

Now that you are aware of the two methods of accounting, let's begin our discussion of accounting for special orders by breaking it into a series of five steps.

Step 1: Create a Sales Order
A special order for merchandise means that there is no stock of that item in the store at the time, so the store owner must create a *sales order*. A sales order (like the one in Figure 8-1 on the following page) is a source document used to record a customer's order for a product that the store does not have in stock but that it can order for the customer. It is a document that will associate the individual customer to an order they placed so when the item(s) come in, the order can be filled for that customer.

Figure 8-1

Sales Order	S/O #W00222			
Date 9/1/XXXX				
Customer Name: Customer A				
Item #	Description	Quantity Ordered	Cost	Price
#WR235	Cream Sofa Vendor X	1	$1,100	$2,000
#WR236	Ottoman Vendor X	1	$250	$500
Totals			$1,350	$2,500

Notice that the sales order is complete with sales order number, date of order, customer name, item numbers, item description, and quantity that the customer ordered, as well as cost of merchandise ordered, price, and totals of that merchandise. This order helps company owners know how many items customers want to order, since it will reflect an item in the company's inventory. However, there is no accounting in the sales or accounts receivable accounts at this point because no merchandise has been received. In accounting terms for accrual accounting, you would say *revenue is not recognized until it is earned.*

Step 2: Prepare a Sales Invoice
The merchandise is now in stock, so a sales invoice is prepared for the sales order (see the sample in Figure 8-2 on the following page). Once the order is officially an invoice, the merchandise that has been reserved for that customer is processed on the invoice and reduced from stock. Notice that sales is not credited

in this case because the customer only paid a deposit on the merchandise that has been received. However, inventory and cost of goods sold accounts are increased by the *cost* of the merchandise, as shown in the Figure 8-2 journal entry below. (Remember, the items are sold at a markup price, but the original receipt is at cost for the items the company purchases to sell.)

Figure 8-2

Date: 10/1/XXXX		
	Debit	**Credit**
Inventory	$1,350	
Cost of Goods		$1,350
Memo: S/O #00222		

Figure 8-3

Sales Invoice			Invoice #9250	
Customer Name: Customer A			S/O #00222	
Date: 10/1/XXXX				
Code	**Item Description**	**Quantity**	**Cost**	**Price**
Inv #WR245	Coffee Table Vendor W	1	$900	$2,000
Inv #WR 246	Sofa Vendor R	1	$450	$500
Tax				$210
Totals			$1,350	$2,710

When a customer makes a deposit on the merchandise, a journal entry is made to account for the customer deposit that was made (see Figure 8-4 below). It goes through your NKS portion of the LINKS figure.

Figure 8-4

Date: 10/1/XXXX		
	Debit	**Credit**
Cash	$500	
Customer Deposits		$500
Memo: Batch 200		

The down payment is placed in a *holding account*, called "customer deposits." Remember from our discussion in chapter 7 that this is actually a liability account because it is something that the company owes to the customer but has not yet received. When that same customer makes another down payment, the journal entry will look like Figure 8-5 (below).

Figure 8-5

Date: 11/1/XXXX		
	Debit	**Credit**
Cash	$500	
Customer Deposits		$500
Memo: Batch 250		

Note how the date of entry is shown. This is important so you have the ability to backtrack to when the customer paid a deposit. Also, in the memo section, it outlines the batch number. Remember, as explained in chapter 4, the batch number is useful when you reconcile your business checking and accounts receivable accounts or to check for lost deposits.

Step 3: Record the Final Deposit

Now that the sales order has been paid in full with a final deposit, here is how the accounting transaction will be recorded for the final deposit (see Figure 8-6 below).

Figure 8-6

Date: 12/1/XXXX		
	Debit	**Credit**
Cash	$1,500	
Customer Deposits		$1,500
Memo: Batch 300		

Step 4: Enter Revenue in Sales and Accounts Receivable

Since the deposits have been received for this invoice, that means the goods have also been received, so *revenue has been earned* and sales and accounts receivable are now credited and debited. Their respective cash receipts and sales journals in the LINKS figure are now linked with this transaction. Figure 8-7 shows the resulting journal entry.

Figure 8-7

Date: 12/1/XXXX		
	Debit	**Credit**
Accounts Receivable	$2,500	
Sales		$2,500
Memo: To Record Sale of and Customer Deposits for Customer A's Invoice #9250 Dated 10/1/XXXX, and Applicable Sales Tax		

Step 5: Clear Out Customer Account

Finally, customer deposits are cleared, as well as accounts receivable (see the journal entry in Figure 8-8 below). This is due to the fact that the customer has paid for the entire order and the order is complete. Now the accounts receivable account for that customer will be zero, and a sale has been recorded.

Figure 8-8

Date: 12/1/XXXX		
	Debit	**Credit**
Customer Deposits	$2,500	
Accounts Receivable		$2,500
Memo: To Record Sale of and Customer Deposits for Customer A's Invoice #9250 Dated 10/1/XXXX, and Applicable Sales Tax		

The accounts receivable and sales transaction have been entered and the pending sale is complete, so it can be put through your profit and loss statement to reflect the actual sale. A journal entry is also created to record the sales tax the customer paid for the merchandise (see Figure 8-9).

Figure 8-9

Date: 12/1/XXXX		
	Debit	**Credit**
Interest Expense	$210	
Sales Tax payable		$210
Memo: To Record 8.4% Sales Tax on Customer A's Invoice #9250 Dated 10/1/XXXX		

A Clear Picture in the General Ledger

The general ledger gives a better picture of how your accounts look once the transaction is complete (see the charts in Figure 8-10 on pages 104–106).

Figure 8-10

General Ledger
Company XYX
For period 10/1/XXXX-12/1/XXXX

1002 Cash

Type	Date	Name	Memo	Split	Debit	Credit	Balance
Check	10/1/ xxxx	Deposit	Batch 200	2800 Customer Deposits	$500		$500
Check	11/1/ xxxx	Deposit	Batch 250	2800 Customer Deposits	$500		$1,000
Check	12/1/ xxxx	Deposit	Batch 300	2800 Customer Deposits	$1,500		$2,500

1200 Inventory

Type	Date	Name	Memo	Split	Debit	Credit	Balance
Sales	12/1/ xxxx	Customer A	Invoice #9250	5000 Cost of Goods Sold		$1,350	$1,350

1400 Accounts Receivable

Type	Date	Name	Memo	Split	Debit	Credit	Balance
Invoice	12/1/xxxx	Customer A	To record sale of and customer deposits for Customer A's Invoice #9250 dated 10/1/xxxx, plus applicable sales tax.	4000 Sales	$2,500		$2,500
Invoice	12/1/xxxx	Customer A	To record sale of and customer deposits for Customer A's Invoice #9250 dated 10/1/xxxx, plus applicable sales tax.	2800 Customer Deposits		$2,500	$0

2800 Customer Deposits

Type	Date	Name	Memo	Split	Debit	Credit	Balance
Payment	11/1/xxxx	Customer A	Batch 200	Cash 1002	$500		$500
Payment	12/1/xxxx	Customer A	Batch 250	Cash 1002	$500		$1,000
Payment	12/1/xxxx	Customer A	Batch 300	Cash 1002	$1,500		$2,500
Invoice	12/1/xxxx	Customer A	To record sale of and customer deposits for Customer A's Invoice #9250 dated 10/1/xxxx, plus applicable sales tax.	1400 Accounts Receivable		$2,500	$0

4000 Sales

Type	Date	Name	Memo	Split	Debit	Credit	Balance
Invoice	12/1/ xxxx	Customer A	To record sale of and customer deposits for Customer A's Invoice #9250 dated 10/1/ xxxx, plus applicable sales tax.	1400 Accounts Receivable		$2,500	$2,500

5000 Cost of Goods Sold

Type	Date	Name	Memo	Split	Debit	Credit	Balance
Sales	12/1/ xxxx	Customer A	Invoice #9250	1200 Inventory	$1,350		$1,350

6000 Interest Expense

Type	Date	Name	Memo	Split	Debit	Credit	Balance
Invoice	12/1/ xxxx	Customer A	To record 8.4% sales tax on Customer A's Invoice #9250 dated 10/1/xxxx	2000 Sales Tax Payable	$210		$210

The general ledger provides the most valuable way to see the transactions that have been processed. If you picture the journals, they hold all the same information, although they are not as easy to follow as the general ledger, which provides the individual accounts' specific debits and credits. In addition, the general ledger shows the "split" account—the reference the general ledger gives you to the other account side of the transaction (in your T-account) that has been either debited or credited in the journal entry for that transaction. The actual debits or credits shown are the entries made for each particular account in the general ledger for that day's transaction entry. Also, remember that in the LINKS figure all the transactions go to the general ledger in detail, so if there is ever a mistake in entering a customer's deposit, or any other transaction, you can find it easily in the general ledger and correct it once you see where the transaction has been placed. As you can see, you will save more time and be more efficient in your accounting processing if you understand how to use the general ledger to your advantage in these and other situations.

Watch Your Dates

An important aspect to remember and understand clearly in accounting for special orders is the dates as indicated through the accounts receivable process. The invoice should be changed for the final deposit. Otherwise, when you pay your sales taxes for the merchandise, you will be paying more than you actually owe. To explain it more clearly, look at Figure 8-3 on page 100, the sales invoice for the special order example, again. The date of this invoice is 10/1/XXXX. However, the date that the final deposit was paid for this invoice was 12/1/XXXX. The date you would be recognizing that the sale was made is 12/1/XXXX, the same date the journal entry was made for accounts receivable and sales. If you have a computerized accounting system, you will have to manually go in and change the date of that invoice to 12/1/XXXX, since the system will automatically keep the date as the original date, 10/1/XXXX. I stress this for two reasons: First, to follow accrual accounting rules, you must not record the sale until revenue is earned. Second, you must realize that if you did not list the sale as pending, and paid sales tax on 10/1/

XXXX, you will have paid for a sale that has not taken place yet, thus overinflating your sales and causing you to pay a higher tax than you actually owe at that time.

Cash Sales

Special orders are used when products are not in stock, but another way of accounting for cash receipts is when customers buy items that are already in stock. For example, if a customer bought some furniture "off the shelf" at an interior design store, the sales invoice would look like Figure 8-11.

Figure 8-11

Sales Receipt			Receipt #4555598		
Customer Name: Customer T					
Date: 10/1/XXXX					
Code	**Item Description**	**Quantity**	**Cost**	**Price**	
Inv #BTXR334	Dining Table Vendor V	1	$700	$1,000	
Inv #BTXX562	Dining Table Chairs Vendor V	1	$500	$850	
Totals			$1,200	$1850	
Tax				$155.40	
Payment				($2005.40)	
Balance				$0.00	

Notice in Figure 8-11 that the source document for this transaction is a sales receipt. Whenever a customer pays in full for merchandise, it is considered a cash sale and a sales receipt is filled out and processed. Also, the merchandise is completely paid for, thus a simple journal entry will record the transaction involved (see Figure 8-12 below).

Figure 8-12

Date: 10/1/XXXX		
	Debit	**Credit**
Cash	$2,005.40	
Sales		$2,005.40
Memo: Customer T Invoice #9850		

Also remember the cost of goods sold and inventory accounts are recorded as the cost of the items, not the sales price. For a review of the journal entry used, see Figure 8-2 on page 100.

Nonprofit donations or charitable contributions are another type of cash sale. A sales receipt is also required for this type of sale. For the simple journal entry, both cash and sales are recorded (see Figure 8-13).

Figure 8-13

Date: 5/1/XXXX		
	Debit	**Credit**
Cash	$350	
Sales: Donations		$350
Memo: Receipt #9583465		

Service Sales

What if you're a service company? How do you account for cash receipts if your business has no inventory? As we discussed in the beginning of this chapter, the only part of the LINKS approach that is used in the transaction processing for service sales is NKS (necessary other journal entries, keeping cash receipts, and sales). For a service sales transaction, a simple sales invoice is set up without inventory on it, showing the service that has been performed for the customer. Similar to the cash donations entry, the journal entry recording this sale is shown in Figure 8-14:

Figure 8-14

Date: 9/1/XXXX		
	Debit	**Credit**
Accounts Receivable	$200	
Sales: Consulting		$200
Memo: Invoice #25973		

Other than the obvious, there are some differences in service transactions versus credit-based ones. For one, there is no sales order or merchandise and no inventory or cost of goods sold journal entries. A similarity, however, is that an invoice serves as the source document. In a service-based business, most accounts receivable transactions involve an invoice because services performed are not usually paid for the same day they are invoiced.

Accounting for Customer Deposits

Up to this point, I have revealed that accounts receivable can be somewhat complicated but can be made simpler by following a few simple steps when encountering credit-type (as opposed to cash) sales. Additionally, I have educated you on the simple way of recording cash sales. In this section, I will go back to the customer deposit part of this chapter, reminding you of the memo designation with each journal entry. Here you will discover how to account for customer deposits most effectively so you can reconcile accounts receivable.

Customers will always be present in any business—hopefully in a continuous flow. You will feel much more in control of the company if those customers are documented accurately and if you, as the business owner, understand all aspects of accounting for them. So let's explore accounting for customer deposits.

As I documented in the examples in the Special Orders section, a customer made many payments on different dates for the same invoice. Now I am going to expand this thought into more customers making deposits on the same day that Customer A did. Figure 8-15 below outlines a typical scenario of different customers depositing money for their invoices on the same day:

Figure 8-15

Customer A	Deposit	10/1/XXXX	$500
Customer B	Deposit	10/1/XXXX	$500
Customer C	Deposit	10/1/XXXX	$225
Total Deposit from Customers		10/1/XXXX	$1,225

All the customers together deposited a total of $1,225. How is this going to be recorded in the most effective way? Let's look at Figure 8-16 and see.

Figure 8-16

Date: 10/1/XXXX		
	Debit	**Credit**
Cash	$1,225	
Customer Deposits		$1,225
Memo: Batch 335		

Obviously, cash is debited since it is increasing from money customers are giving the company, and customer deposits is credited since it is decreasing by the individual amounts on the invoices for each customer. What I want to highlight as the most valuable information in this transaction, however, is simply the memo. If you remember from chapter 4 when I gave you some ways to put "language" into your numbers by memos, this is an example that will shed more light on this topic. Notice the memo spells out "Batch 335." Why is this so important? This batch number notation separates this money to solely the customers who deposited cash receipts for this particular day. While it may not make sense now, it will as we move to the reconciling stage (an important skill to learn, as most companies desire to reconcile their accounts receivable but fall short of doing so simply because they do not know how to simplify the process). Moving on, make sure this batch is prepared separately from any other monies received for the day. This step is a significantly important one for the reconciliation process to work properly.

Once the deposit has been recorded in the books, it will automatically be generated into the general ledger, as defined earlier in the book. Both accounts, as depicted, will zero each other out if looking at the debit versus credit. Notice the Batch 335 memo identifies the connection with the two accounts. The process will be simple as long as you follow the steps of batching the deposit, preparing this deposit separate from any other money received in a given day, and reconciling accounts receivable either at the end of a week, month, year, or however often the accounts receivable account is reconciled.

Other benefits to the process are that if money is missing from a deposit, the problem can be backtracked and more easily identified as to who made the deposit and what day it was made due to what the difference was of cash deposited and accounts receivable recorded. The receipts process also works the same way for credit card receipts. It is all the same, as long as the money is treated as cash on the company's accounting record. Customers are the lifeblood of your business; if there is not proper accounting done, especially a process that makes sense to the people who operate it, the company will be in jeopardy.

For Those Special Circumstances

There are special circumstances and events that exist in every company. While there may be customers who don't pay for their orders within the year, returned merchandise, discounts for invoices paid early, or sales tax that is off on invoices, all are relevant to the accounting process and must be recorded. Let's tackle one at a time.

Sales Tax Discrepancies

Sometimes there are sales tax discrepancies in a company's

paperwork. Let's say that when a customer ordered some items, the sales tax on the invoice was calculated on the order manually (before being entered into a computer financial software program) as $142.72. However, upon data entry into the computer program, that same invoice was calculated at $142.74. The customer has already received and paid for their order, but there is a difference of $.02. How do you bring the books into balance?

The order can be fixed by showing that the customer paid the entire balance on the invoice (even though it was off by two cents). When the deposit is put through for that invoice, an offset account, also known as an *expense* (which is really an expense to the company because it is incurring the expense for the difference), will be debited. Creating an over and short account (see Figure 8-17) gives you the ability to manage accounts receivable in such situations.

Figure 8-17

Date: 1/1/XXXX		
	Debit	**Credit**
Cash	$1,841.72	
Accounts Receivable		$1,841.74
Over and short	$ .02	
Memo: Batch 450		

Slow-Paying Customers

Some companies have slow-paying customers, even customers who do not pay within the year. Technically speaking, accounts that are overdue by a year should be deemed uncollectible. Larger companies with many accounts receivable are more likely to have overdue accounts receivable instead of small companies, simply because the larger companies cannot manage calling customers on a regular basis, unless, of course, there is someone who strictly handles customer account calls. Accounting for such customers is nevertheless necessary to close the books at the end of the company's year. I recommend doing what is called a *reclass to bad debts expense*. Also touched on in chapter 4, this simple memo will help you distinguish specific types of transactions and move them, if needed. When you reclass an amount, you move it from one account to another. How it is done for accounts receivable is in this fashion?

The start of the reclass begins in the transaction displayed in Figure 8-18 (below). Cash is debited, and accounts receivable is credited to clear the remaining balance out of this customer's account.

Figure 8-18

Date: 12/31/XXXX		
	Debit	**Credit**
Cash	$250	
Accounts Receivable		$250
Memo: Reclass Customer N Balance to Bad Debts		

Next, the cash will be cleared, and the accounts receivable balance will be moved into the bad debts expense account (as shown in Figure 8-19 on the next page).

Figure 8-19

Date: 12/31/XXXX		
	Debit	**Credit**
Bad Debt Expense	$250	
Cash		$250
Memo: Reclass Customer N Balance to Bad Debts		

By using this type of accounting, if bad debts are looked up at a later date on your company's financial statements, a true picture of the journal entries will be evident. In the same manner, if customer balances are not cleared within the year, instead of using the bad debts expense account, a prior period expense account (also discussed in chapter 4) would be used to clear the balance along with the cash account.

Early-Bird Discounts
Many companies have incentives for customers to pay off their invoices early. Terms like "2 percent net 30," which means if payment is paid within thirty days, the customer can pay the invoice price less 2 percent of the order. Take the situation where Customer O has an invoice dated 5/1/XXXX that has a balance of $3,500 and terms 2 percent net 30. Customer O decides to pay for the entire invoice early on 5/25/XXXX. Figure 8-20 (see the following page) shows the journal entry to record that. Notice that accounts receivable must be reduced by the amount net the discount. In addition, cash is only debited for the amount of the invoice less the 2 percent discount, which is a subaccount of sales since the discount has been honored for Customer O.

Figure 8-20

Date: 5/25/XXXX		
	Debit	**Credit**
Cash	$3,430	
Accounts Receivable		$3,430
Memo: Batch 4500		

Another journal entry to record the actual sale is made, with the sales account credited for the entire amount of sale (see Figure 8-21 below). This is because the actual sale is tied to the inventory that has been reserved for the customer and must be cleared in its entirety when posted. In addition, the sales discount will be debited to offset the sale amount, thus posting in the income statement as a net balance. Just remember that the sales account is tied into receiving the inventory or service. If it is netted when posted, it will not be accurate in the income statement.

Figure 8-21

Date: 5/25/XXXX		
	Debit	**Credit**
Accounts Receivable	$3,430	
Sales Discounts	$70	
Sales		$3,500

Write-Offs

Sometimes customers do not use their discounts. These types of transactions are called *write-offs*, and they were another one of the memos discussed in chapter 4. Remember, write-offs are considered entries that represent anything that occurs to clear something off of a customer's account. A couple of journal entries are required to move this transaction to its proper account (see Figure 8-22).

Figure 8-22

Date: 8/1/XXXX		
	Debit	**Credit**
Cash	$50	
Sales Discounts		$50
Memo: Write-off of Customer N's Discount		

Date: 8/1/XXXX		
	Debit	**Credit**
Sales Discounts	$50	
Cash		$50
Memo: Write-off of Customer N's Discount		

Customer Returns

No company is ever exempt from customers who do not like a product or service and thus return the sale. See Figures 8-23 and 8-24 on pages 119 and 120, respectively, for how a product or service return is recorded.

Figure 8-23

Credit Memo		CM#5585	
Customer R			
Date 6/4/XXXX			
Code	**Item Description**	**Quantity**	**Price**
Inv. #W266	Ottoman Vendor X	1	$255
TX Sales Tax Payable			$21.42
Credit			$276.42

Initially, the credit memo paperwork is completed for Customer R. A credit memo is a document that signifies credit to a customer for something they already purchased. At the same time, Customer R's sales invoice will be credited for the amount of the item as indicated.

Figure 8-24

Credit Memo	CM#5585
Sales Invoice	Invoice #9880
Customer R	
Date 1/1/XXXX	

Code	Item Description	Quantity	Price
Inv #W262	Lamp Vendor R	1	$300
Inv #W263	Side Chair Vendor X	1	$200
Inv #W266	Ottoman Vendor X	1	$255
TX Sales Tax Payable			$63.42
Total			$818.42
Payment			$818.42
Credit Memo			$(276.42)

Accounting for the credit is going to come out of sales and sales tax payable. On the journal entry, sales are reduced for the product returned. Additionally, sales tax payable is debited to reduce the amount of sales taxes due, and cash is credited to pay Customer R back for what was returned.

Figure 8-25

6/4/XXXX		
	Debit	**Credit**
Sale	$250	
Sales Tax Payable	$21.42	
Cash		$276.42
Memo: Credit Memo 5585		

Returns can take different forms as well. However, this type is the most commonly used, and it is not within the scope of this book to expand on other types here.

Factoring Accounts Receivable for Cash Flow

Pledging (factoring) of accounts receivable is the final type of accounts receivable transaction processing we are going to discuss. Pledging accounts receivable is something companies do when they are in need of more cash flow. They will "pledge" or sell their accounts receivable to a factoring company. This factor, as it is called, will then receive all accounts receivable payments. The factor will then pay the company a certain percentage of the accounts receivable. When the factor does this, he will send the company a list of all the accounts receivable customers he paid, amounts paid, and the corresponding invoice numbers. There is usually a certain percentage of the accounts receivable balance—often 80 percent or so—that the factoring company will pay to you immediately. The other 20 percent of the accounts receivable—less 2 percent or so, depending on what the factoring company agrees to pay you—will be paid once you have entirely paid off your order. This is the service charge for processing your company's accounts receivables.

When doing the accounting for this process, you would set up your customers the same as you would in any other customer type of transaction. The only difference is you will not be collecting all the money the customer owes to you. Instead, they will pay the factoring company directly. Take the scenario presented in Figure 8-26 (on the following page).

For the initial sale, you will record the customer's purchase, as well as the inventory and cost of goods sold for the cost of the merchandise.

Figure 8-26

Customer P	Bought $700 worth of merchandise	10/1/XXXX
Customer Q	Bought $1000 worth of merchandise	10/1/XXXX
Customer R	Bought $300 worth of merchandise	10/1/XXXX

6/1/XXXX		
	Debit	**Credit**
Accounts Receivable	$700	
Sales		$700
Memo: Customer P		
6/1/XXXX		
	Debit	**Credit**
Accounts Receivable	$1,000	
Sales		$1,000
Memo: Customer Q		
6/1/XXXX		
	Debit	**Credit**
Accounts Receivable	$300	
Sales		$300
Memo: Customer R		
6/1/XXXX		
	Debit	**Credit**
Inventory	$900	
Cost of Goods Sold		$900
Memo: Invoice 4958		
On 10/5/XXXX, Customer P paid $600 to the factoring company, leaving $100 balance in their account.		
On 10/20/XXXX, Customer Q paid $600 to the factoring company, leaving $400 balance in their account.		
On 10/31/XXXX, Customer R paid $100 to the factoring company, leaving $200 balance in their account.		

The factoring company usually sets specific dates on which you will be paid. For the example in Figure 8-28 (see the following page), the factoring company pays at the beginning of every month. They will pay up to 80 percent of the receivables, which is $560 for Customer P (80 percent of $700), $600 for Customer Q, and $100 for Customer R—or $1,260, the total of all deposits for the month of October. As demonstrated in Figure 8-27 (below), the company selling the accounts receivable will then make a journal entry batch for these customers, which will be placed into their respective individual accounts, thus reducing them to their remaining balances.

Figure 8-27

11/1/XXXX		
	Debit	**Credit**
Cash	$1,260	
Accounts Receivable		$1,260
Memo: Credit Memo 5585		

When the following month arrives, all the customers pay their remaining balances. Now, since the factor only pays the company 98 percent of its accounts receivable (remember that the service charge is 2 percent of the sale), the company will still have 2 percent of the customer's balance left on their books. There will first be a journal entry to record customers' final receipts. Customer P's receipt is $126 ($686, or 98 percent of the $560 initial 80 percent payment), Customer Q's receipt is $380 ($980, or 98 percent of the $600 initial payment), Customer R's receipt is $194 ($294, or 98 percent of the $100 initial payment). The journal entry to record the rest of the receipts in total is shown in Figure 8-28 on the following page.

Figure 8-28

12/1/XXXX		
	Debit	**Credit**
Cash	$700	
Accounts Receivable		$700
Memo: Batch 341		

Notice that the total deposits for the customers is $1,960, or 98 percent of the total customer receipts ($1,260 + $700). The remaining 2 percent is cleared out of the customer's accounts as a factoring expense. To clear out the remaining balance requires two journal entries like the ones in Figure 8-29.

Figure 8-29

12/1/XXXX		
	Debit	**Credit**
Cash	$40	
Accounts Receivable		$40
Memo: Reclass Factor Fee to Factor Expense		

12/1/XXXX		
	Debit	**Credit**
Factor Expense	$40	
Cash		$40
Memo: Reclass Factor Fee to Factor Expense		

Remember when I talked about reclassing accounts? This is a good example of how you would clear out your remaining balance in your customers' accounts and move it into an expense account to properly report for this irregular transaction. Please also note that these types of cash receipts can either be on a cash or accrual basis. In this example, I used a cash basis because it will be easier to use the cash basis for pledging receivables due to the factor fees involved.

Sinking In?

I hope you are beginning to understand the first three LINKS journals we have discussed. As you can see, your accounts receivable is a major portion of your transaction processing in accounting. In addition, remember that the cash receipts cycle can be processed either with inventory (in which all the LINKS are used) or without inventory (where only the NKS portion is in play). When you keep the LINKS together and follow the process I have outlined, your cash receipts and sales operations will run smoothly and without error. Accounting really is a simple process; it is just a matter of focusing on your accounts of higher importance to see how easy accounting can be for you and anyone else who is trying to understand it.

Chapter Eight:
What's the Point?

This chapter is vital in your understanding of accounting.

+ This chapter discusses accounts receivable and sales, the two highest transaction-generating accounts in the LINKS system (other than inventory) that together make up a customer's purchases.

+ In the process of accounts receivable, all the LINKS come into play. For the cash receipts cycle, two different versions of the LINKS approach are used. With inventory, all the LINKS are used; without inventory, only the NKS portion of the LINKS is used.

Special orders is one way of accounting for goods.

+ Remember when a customer is purchasing something that is not in stock at the store, it must be recorded as a credit sale or accounts receivable.

‣ *Accrual accounting,* defined as a method of accounting the recognized expenses when incurred and revenues when earned regardless of when cash is received, is a special part of accounting for special orders.

+ For special orders, the sale will stay "pending" and not post until the order is complete.

+ Cash sales are different, recognizing a sale when cash is received.

There are several steps when accounting for special orders.

+ First, create a sales order. This is a nonposting document listing customer name, date of order, order number, and

item(s) ordered with quantities, description, and price and
cost listed.

+ Second, you must create a sales invoice. Once merchandise
is in stock, a sales invoice is created, reserved merchandise
is processed on the invoice, and items are reduced from
stock. A journal entry for inventory and cost of goods
sold is made at this time. The customer's down payment
is placed in a holding account, called customer deposits. A
journal entry for inventory and cost of goods sold is also
made at this time.

+ Step three is recording the final deposit. Be careful
to change the invoice to reflect the final deposit date.
Otherwise, when you pay your sales/excise taxes, you will
be paying more than you actually owe.

+ For the fourth step, revenue is entered in the LINKS cash
receipts and sales journal. This deposit will record the
actual sale debiting accounts receivable and crediting sales
since the order is now complete. (Remember the accrual
accounting rules.)

+ The final step is to clear out the customer's account. Now
that the customer has paid in full, accounts receivable
is cleared for that customer, and the customer deposit
account is also cleared as well.

+ Remember in the LINKS figure that all transactions go to
the general ledger in detail so if there is ever a mistake in
entering a customer's deposit or any other transaction, you
can find it easily in the general ledger and correct it once
you see when the transaction was placed.

Another way of accounting for goods is cash sales.

- Cash sales are only applicable when a customer is buying something that is already in stock.
- The cash and sales account automatically record the sale, as well as cost of goods sold and inventory (if applicable) but not customer deposits.

There are several notes about customer deposits.

- Accounting for many customer orders on the same day takes the *special order* for merchandise to a different level.
- To record deposits of more than one customer in a day, a batch of all customer deposits is made, recording the total of all the customers' deposits for the day, with a memo notation giving a batch number to this deposit.
- The batch should be prepared separately from any other money received for that day.
- If money needs to be backtracked, the memo and batch number provide a good reference to find the deposit.

There may be sales tax discrepancies and these must be addressed.

- Sometimes when a customer pays for their invoice, the paper copy amount does not match what the computerized system calculates the total as. This can lead to totals being off by small amounts.
- To handle the discrepancies, an over and short account will be charged for the difference.

You must account for slow-paying customers.

- When a customer does not pay for their order within the year, a reclass of that invoice to bad debts should be done to get it off of the books.

+ Bad debts expense is debited and the accounts receivable account cleared out for the total of the customer's balance(s).

Discounts for paying off orders early must be handled appropriately.

+ In the case of paying off orders early, accounts receivable must be reduced by the amount net the discount.
+ The rest goes to the sales discounts account, an account in the sales portion of the income statement.
+ If the customer does not use the discount, a write-off is done, clearing the discount to the sales account.

Customer returns must be accounted for.

+ When customers return merchandise, a source document called a *credit memo* is required to account for the return.
+ Sales and sales tax payable are both affected for the portion of the merchandise returned, and the sales tax applicable to the item(s) returned.

Factoring accounts receivable is something companies do when they are in need of more cash flow.

+ Also called "pledging," this is the process of selling accounts receivable to a factoring company.
+ The factor pays the company selling its receivables a certain percentage of the total receivables it obtains, usually 80 percent or so. The other 20 percent less 2 percent or so will be paid back to the company once the orders are paid in full.
+ The 2 percent is the service fee the factoring company charges you.

9

Something Borrowed, Something Owed:
Using the Accounts Payable Cycle in the LINKS Approach

We have arrived at the final cycle: the accounts payable cycle. If you recall from previous chapters, grasping accounting has to do largely with understanding the cycles that operate together. This final cycle is much less complex but equally important in our accounting lesson. In this cycle, along with inventory always comes accounts payable, also a corresponding portion of the LINKS approach defined on page 73. Accounts payable is defined as all merchandise, services, or expenses that are owed to someone else, and is specifically designated as a liability to the company that is receiving the accounts payable. Accounts payable is always a liability since it represents something owed. Furthermore, it is in the company's best interest to keep accounts payable at a minimum so the cash flow is not always inundated with paying the bills. Accounts payable uses the LIN portion of the LINKS figure—liabilities owed, inventory reserved, and necessary journal entries (also stated as liabilities owed for vendors, inventory reserved for customers, and necessary other journal entries). In Figure 9-1 are the LINKS in the journals block that are part of the accounts payable cycle (see below). In this chapter, we'll take a look at this processing cycle.

Figure 9-1

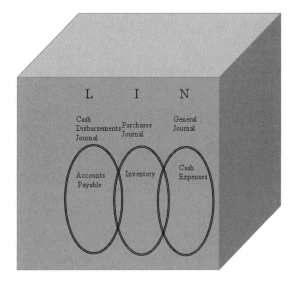

Inventory

Why does accounts payable have any relation to inventory when inventory is merchandise? As touched on in earlier chapters, accounts payable has a direct link to inventory: Whenever inventory is received at a company, an invoice comes in. That invoice goes directly to the accounts payable division since it will most often be paid at a later date. Following that, the invoice is looked at and then entered into the accounting system. The items for inventory will be received, which will create a debit on the inventory side for the total of the merchandise received and a credit to the accounts payable for the total invoice debt that is due.

Expenses

Now there is clarity on the link of accounts payable to inventory, but how is it also related to expenses? Quite simply, expenses are always abounding in a business, and accounts payable is the avenue into which expenses are entered. Expenses are part of the general journal of the LINKS diagram. Take, for example, an accounts payable invoice for rent for the next month. The initial entry would be a credit to accounts payable and a debit to rent expense. Consequently that rent expense is now formally a part of the income statement for that year. The accounts payable invoice, however, will get paid eventually. Once the accounts payable invoice for the rent is paid, the cash account will be credited to pay it, and the accounts payable account will be debited to clear out the invoice. This explains the connection between accounts payable and expenses.

Credit Card Expenses

Another liability account in accounts payable is for the credit cards that the owner or employee owns. These are company credit cards for business purchases or expenses, which can also include inventory. These cards help the business keep better track of the expenses and purchases it is making. For any business, it is a good idea to have any employee or owner set up an *expense report* to track monthly expenses that go on these cards. Setting up the expenses on a spreadsheet can work quite well. The expenses are broken down on the spreadsheet by category, then entered into the financial records by each expense. The expense report is then turned in at the beginning of each month. If done monthly, the company will have a great track record of what the employee or employer is using the credit card for and can catch and prevent overspending or personal spending on the card more quickly.

Cash

In every one of the LINKS journal accounts, the cash account (part of the general journal) has been a piece of the process (the N in LINKS). For any cash payment or receipt, cash is in the picture. Cash is important since it is the actual money that goes out to pay for the items or expenses and is increased by the cash receipts and sales of the merchandise the company sells. Cash is also tied into the other aspects outside the LINKS diagram, which I will discuss later.

This chapter focused on the final LINKS cycle—the accounts payable cycle. As you saw, the accounts payable cycle relates to all credit-type invoices and expenses that are a part of a company's everyday business operations. This cycle is much less complex than the two discussed in the previous chapters, since it is much more straightforward as to the types of transactions that are involved in it. In addition, because the transactions do not vary much in this cycle, it is much easier to understand. You are now in the final stretch of grasping accounting, hopefully seeing it more clearly. In our next few chapters I will be talking about the LINKS set apart from the cycles, otherwise called "standalone LINKS."

Chapter Nine:
What's the Point?

Accounts payable is defined as merchandise, services, or expenses that are owed to someone else.

+ Owners should keep accounts payable at a minimum so cash flow is not inundated with paying bills.

Expenses have a connection to the accounts payable cycle.

+ Most of your expenses will come in the form of invoices for rent, utility bills, insurance payments, etc., which will be paid at a later date. These all represent your accounts payable.

Your cash account plays an important role.

+ In this cycle it is the account credited when accounts payable invoices are paid for.

10

The Link Stands Alone, Part 1:
Asset Accounts in the General Journal

Up until now I have shown you the accounts from the chart of accounts that make up most of the transaction processing in your business, which must be understood well in order for you to understand the language of accounting. In review, I have touched on accounts receivable (A/R), inventory, and accounts payable (A/P), where the bulk of all transactions occur. In addition, they are correlated to more than one of the links in the LINK figure. A/R without inventory is NKS, A/P is LIN, and A/R with inventory is LINKS. I have stressed the importance of learning these LINKS and the accounts that make them up in order for you to be comfortable with the vast majority of your accounting processing. Let me assure you that if you understand how these links correlate, you will be on your way to realizing that accounting is not a foreign language; you can do it yourself.

In this chapter, I am now moving on to the link that can stand alone in special situations: the general journal. Instead of a cycle that runs to keep your accounting recorded accurately, there are special types of transactions unique to your business that must be recorded and are processed through a journal entry only. A cycle is not involved since the journal entries are separate transactions that do not affect any other LINKS, hence the definition of the N link—other journal entries. For reference purposes, I am outlining these asset accounts according to their place in the chart of accounts, but remember each transaction will be unique to your business. As the situation arises, you will need to determine what journal entries are appropriate for that particular case. In Figure 10-1 below, you will see the asset accounts in the general journal link. Let's start our discussion with prepaid accounts.

Figure 10-1

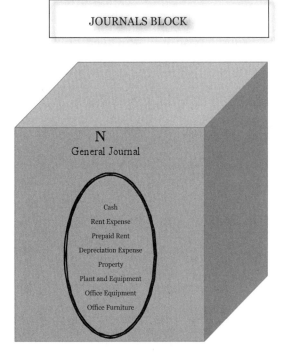

Prepaid Accounts

Prepaid accounts are used to pay for something in advance. It is an asset to the company since it represents something the company owns. Many companies pay their rent through prepaid accounts so they are not late and thus avoid late fees. This account is debited initially for the amount of an ongoing expense. At the end of the year, the account is then credited for whatever unused amount is left and offset by the expense it is associated with. In other words, the account represents an activity that spans more than one period (a year). A journal entry to document a typical prepaid transaction process is shown in Figure 10-2 below. The journal entry shows the initial transaction to prepay for the rent. Prepaid rent is debited since it is paid in advance, and cash is credited for the payment.

Figure 10-2

7/1/XXXX		
	Debit	**Credit**
Prepaid rent	$12,000	
Cash		$12,000
Memo: To Record Annual Rent ($12,000/12=$1,000 Per Month)		

Now, let's say at the end of the year the company had only been charged for six months of rent since they prepaid in July. The transaction to show the actual rent expense paid for the year would be set up like Figure 10-3 on the following page. This memo records the actual rent for the six months and will decrease prepaid rent by $6,000, leaving $6,000 in the prepaid rent account for the following year.

Figure 10-3

12/31/XXXX		
	Debit	**Credit**
Rent Expense	$6,000	
Prepaid Rent		$6,000
Memo: Rent Expense for July – December YR XXXX		

Property, Plant, and Equipment

For many companies, the largest dollar category of assets on the balance sheet is long-lived (noncurrent) tangible productive assets, called property, plant, and equipment. These are also referred to as plant or fixed assets. They are considered long-lived assets since they are used for the greatest amount of time. These types of assets include buildings and equipment; some examples are assembly lines, machinery, warehouse buildings, garages, loading docks, office equipment, computers, etc. To determine the costs of these types of assets, you must take into account not just the asset itself but also the cost of getting the asset ready for its intended use. For example, the cost of machinery equipment includes its purchase price (with sales tax), transportation costs, insurance in transit, assembly, installation, testing, painting, etc. Many costs are attributed to plant assets, which in turn help your business qualify for more depreciation expenses on these items.

Office Equipment, Equipment, Computers, Office Furniture

The other category of assets on your balance sheet includes those used inside your business. These types of assets include such items as office desks, office chairs, routers, computers, computer equipment, and cell phones—to name a few. The costs associated with these assets are strictly the purchase price with tax (as well as software purchased for a computer). If there are any set up fees, they will be expensed in their appropriate category in the income statement by type of services provided.

Depreciating Your Assets

When an asset is in the process of being placed into service by a company, the purchase costs have a future benefit and are part of the cost of the asset. These costs are expensed through the process of depreciation over the life of the asset. Note that the depreciation expense itself does not carry forward each year but is closed at the end of each period. There are a number of ways to determine asset depreciation. However, most commonly three main depreciation methods are used, which are based on the following patterns of consumption:

- *Useful life of the asset:* This is the amount of life for which the IRS determines that the asset will be in use.
- *Salvage value:* This is the estimated value the asset will realize at the end of its useful life. Salvage value is used in conjunction with purchase price and accounting method to determine how much the asset depreciates each period. It can be a "best guess" and can be determined by the IRS.
- *Pattern of consumption:* What this means is how the asset's benefits are consumed. Some examples are units produced, kilowatts generated, or miles traveled.

How then do these methods work, and what method works best for your company?

Straight Line Method

This the method used most often and is the easiest to understand. In the straight line method, there is a simple formula to keep track of all depreciable assets:

$$\text{Annual Depreciation Expense} = \text{Cost of Asset} - \text{Salvage Value}$$

Useful Life

Depending on the asset being depreciated, you choose one of three useful life estimations to use in the straight line computation:

- *Buildings and leasehold improvements:* 10–40 years
- *Machinery and equipment:* 5–12 years
- *Furniture and fixtures:* 10 years

What happens, though, when depreciation expenses have to be revised due to wear and tear, inadequacy, improvements to maintenance, or obsolescence? In this case, the book value of the asset (the asset's value on the balance sheet less accumulated depreciation) must be spread over the remaining useful life. The reason for this is that the company's original estimates for salvage value (the amount the asset is worth at the end of its useful life and what you can sell the asset for in case you decide to dispose of it) and useful life were not wrong. Instead, they were based on the best information available at the time. When the new information becomes available, the original estimate is revised from that point forward. For example, if improved maintenance procedures were in place for an aircraft that originally had a useful life of ten years, and it has already been depreciated for ten years, due to the improvements in the plane to extend its useful life, its annual depreciation will be lower. This is simply because the value of the aircraft has increased, and thus its years of service have also increased.

A good way to keep track of a company's equipment is to set it up on a spreadsheet. The chart in figure 10-4 shows how to use the straight-line method of depreciation to keep track of these items.

Figure 10-4

Depreciation Schedule Book

Description	Disposed	Purchase Date	Cost	Life	Mo/ Dep	1/xxxx- 3/xxxx	4/xxxx- 6/xxxx	7/xxxx- 9/xxxx	10/xxxx- 12/xxxx	Net Book Value
Office Equipment, Computers, Software										
Computer		1/xxxx	2000	60	33.33	100	100	100	100	1600
Office Furniture										
Office Computer Desk		4/xxxx	1000	60	16.67		50	50	50	850
Equipment										
Office Phone		1/xxxx	65	60	1.08	3.24	3.24	3.24	3.24	52.04
										Fixed Yr XX
Office Equipment, Computers, Software										400
Office Furniture										150
Equipment										12.96
Total Assets										
Period Depreciation										562.96
Accumulated Depreciation										562.96

Notice how all important information is included in the spreadsheet. At the top row of the spreadsheet is a "Description" column. This is very important for keeping track of your assets individually so you will depreciate the assets correctly. Next to that is a "Disposed" column. This is only used once the asset has been fully depreciated or has been exchanged or sold. You will just mark this column with an *X* once the asset is disposed of. Your next column is the "Purchase Date." This is the date you actually purchased the asset. Again, this is of extreme importance to include since your asset's depreciation calculation will be based on this date. The "Life" column is how long the asset, by IRS rules, is to be completely depreciated. The next column, the "Mo/Dep," means how much depreciation your asset will have per month. The next four columns, "1/XXXX–12/XXXX," represent quarterly depreciation for the assets. You can set it up by month as well, but summing up the totals quarterly condenses the data and makes it easier to read. Finally, the last column is your "Net Book Value," or the value that your asset is worth at the end of the twelve-month period minus depreciation. The rows for each type of equipment are summed together, and the totals for each category are listed at the bottom. To insert additional years you simply add new columns to the right that show the monthly or quarterly depreciation amounts, bring them down to the summary section in an empty column, and add a row for accumulated depreciation. The spreadsheet keeps the depreciation amounts together in an easy-to-read format. It is a great tool for business, since it will keep track of your company's equipment accurately, and you will know when items become fully depreciated by looking at the totals in the equipment categories.

Using the computer data from the depreciation spreadsheet on the previous page, Figure 10-5 shows how to create journal entries for depreciation expenses (below).

Figure 10-5

3/30/XXXX		
	Debit	**Credit**
Depreciation Expense	$100	
Accumulated Depreciation		$100
Memo: Depreciation–Computer 1/1-3/30/XXXX		

To record this journal entry requires only depreciation expenses and accumulated depreciation data. At the end of the year, the total depreciation expense for all assets will be recorded on the income statement, while accumulated depreciation is the offset to the property, plant, and equipment on the balance sheet. When the assets here are deducted from accumulated depreciation, the amount left is the value of these assets after depreciation. You can see that keeping track of all asset depreciation is vital to knowing their worth.

Accelerated Depreciation

This is another method of depreciation. One way of calculating this type of depreciation is to use the double declining balance method. This method uses the straight line rate and doubles it. For example, for equipment that has a five-year life, the straight line rate would be 20 percent (one-fifth) per year. The double declining balance rate would be 40 percent per year. In addition, the rate (40 percent) is multiplied by the book value at the beginning of the year, not the depreciable base. Also note that, unlike other depreciation methods, the salvage value does not apply in calculating the depreciation. However, the asset is still only depreciated down to salvage value. To understand this, an example is shown in Figure 10-6 for equipment that costs $55,000 with a five-year useful life and a salvage value of $5,000.

Figure 10-6

Year	Double Declining Rate X Book Value	Depreciation Expense	Accumulated Depreciation	Book Value
				$55,000
1	(.40 x $55,000)	$22,000	$22,000	$33,000
2	(.40 x $33,000)	$13,200	$35,200	$19,800
3	(.4 x 19,800)	$7,920	$43,120	$11,880
4	(.40 x 11,880)	$4,752	$47,872	$7,128
5	(.4 x $7,128)	$2,851*	$50,723	$4,277

* Note that this amount would change to $2,128, or Year 5 book value minus $5,000, if the expected salvage value were still $5,000.

However, since this method ignores salvage value in the calculations, the actual book value is reduced to $4,277. Also note that the book value at the end of Year 4 was $7,128. This is still not enough to follow the rules of depreciating down to salvage value. The book value has not yet gone down to $5,000 or less, thus the reason for the depreciation in Year 5.

When choosing which depreciation method to use, be aware that tax regulations do not require companies to use the same depreciation methods for both income taxes and financial reporting. What this means is that companies can use the accelerated method of depreciation for tax purposes, which is more difficult to calculate, and use the straight line method for their books. This is a big benefit because companies typically pay fewer income taxes in the early years of an asset's life and more in the later years. For companies that have a large amount of new equipment, using the accelerated method for tax purposes allows them to be able to postpone payments they would otherwise owe up front, thereby allowing them to have more cash flow available to pay off the equipment earlier.

The Modified Accelerated Cost Recovery System (MACRS) was enacted by congress in the Tax Reform Act of 1986, which established the classes of property applicable to this type of accelerated depreciation. The classes of property are divided by the number of years they are to be depreciated per the tax law. For example, the tax law under the MACRS classifies computers, automobiles and light trucks, construction equipment, and research and development property to be classified as seven-year property subject to the 200 percent declining balance method. What this means is that for tax purposes you can use this method for these types of assets to apply more depreciation early on in the asset's stage of depreciation, giving you a larger tax write-off in the first years of the asset's useful life. As mentioned earlier, the point of the IRS regulation is to use it to calculate depreciation for equipment or property for tax purposes. However, for your own company's books, some of the classes will be different. This MACRS method consequently allows the assets to be spread out for more depreciation and less taxes to pay over a longer time period.

Units of Activity Method

This third method of depreciation is used when the benefit of the asset is attributed to an activity (like services provided or number of units manufactured) rather than the passage of time. This method is mostly appropriate for assets that have easily measured benefits. To understand this type of depreciation more clearly, consider this example: You have some equipment that cost you $50,000, the salvage value is $5,000, and it is estimated that the machine will have a life of 100,000 machine hours. Your depreciation per unit is then calculated as $.50 ($50,000/100,000), or cost less salvage value divided by 100,000 machine hours. If production in the years following are 25,000 units for one year and 30,000 units for the next year, then the depreciation expense would be $12,500 for the year of 25,000 units used (25,000 x $.5) and $15,000 for the year of 30,000 units used (30,000 x $.5). This method is most useful for miles driven, trucks, machine hours, or airplanes.

Leasehold Improvements

Another asset that is considered a standalone link is leasehold improvements. These assets can be a little confusing when you are trying to decide which category to put data into. For classification purposes, leasehold improvements are fixtures or furniture attached to real estate, and they come under the *other asset* section of the balance sheet. When a tenant's lease expires, the tenant may remove them as long as they do not damage the property or conflict with the lease. Examples of leasehold improvements are cabinets, light fixtures, window treatments, paintings, and wallpaper. Not only are leasehold improvements amortized over the lease term, but when anything goes wrong with the fixture, the costs associated with the repair are entered under this asset. Let's look at an example:

Tenant A has carpet that is new in her building. There was a water leak and it damaged the carpet. The damage was $1,500. This cost will be associated with the carpet, since the carpet is attached to the building. Figure 10-7 below shows the journal entry.

Figure 10-7

6/1/XXXX		
	Debit	**Credit**
Repair Expense	$1,500	
Leasehold Improvements		$1,500
Memo: Repair to Carpet in Building A		

The cost is deducted from the leasehold improvements, since it is reducing the value of the fixture. When the carpet is replaced, the leasehold improvement will be debited to show the new fixture that was added to the building. (See the resulting journal entry in Figure 10-8 below.)

Figure 10-8

7/1/XXXX		
	Debit	**Credit**
Leasehold improvements	$2,000	
Cash		$2,000
Memo: New Carpet Installed in Building A		

Notice that the leasehold improvement was debited, which increases the total in its corresponding account and decreases cash for the amount paid for the carpet.

Over time, amortization will decrease the total account. The leasehold improvement will be amortized over the shorter life of the improvement or the remaining lease term. Amortization is a little like depreciation since it is offset against the leasehold improvement, but it is not tax deductible. Also, the tenant does not own the leasehold improvement, since it is considered an intangible asset (not something you are able to pick up and take somewhere), because the tenant does not own the property.

This chapter takes you into your first "standalone LINK," separate from the cycles in the previous chapter. The general journal covers a wide variety of asset account journal entries, all quite different and varied—as noted in this chapter. What I want you to clearly grasp in this chapter is that each situation is unique in what assets you will be journaling for your company. Your industry will determine what types of transactions are appropriate for your business. In addition, since this link is not a part of a cycle, and is related to the assets portion of your balance sheet, each transaction can affect any asset, contra asset, or depreciation expense. From this point, I will be discussing more of these standalone LINKS as they associate with certain parts of your balance sheet and income statement.

Chapter Ten:
What's the Point?

The general journal is the link that stands alone.

+ Instead of a cycle that keeps your accounting recorded accurately, there are special types of transactions unique to your business that are recorded by a journal entry only.

+ A cycle is not involved since the journal entries are separate transactions that do not affect any of the other LINKS.

There are several asset accounts with general journal transactions.

* *Prepaid accounts:* These are used to pay for something in advance.

* *Property, plant, and equipment:* These are considered long-lived assets since they are used for the greatest amount of time. Costs for these assets include not only the cost of the asset but also the cost of getting the asset ready for its intended use. Some examples are assembly lines, machinery, or warehouse buildings.

* *Office equipment, computers, office furniture:* This includes assets inside your business. Costs are determined by cost of item only, including sales tax. Some examples are office desks, office chairs, computers, routers, etc.

* *Leasehold improvements:* These are known as furniture or fixtures attached to your real estate. Examples are carpeting, cabinets, light fixtures, etc. Note that any repair or maintenance on these will be directly charged to the leasehold improvements account.

Depreciation of asset accounts is an important concept.

+ Depreciation is based on three things: useful life of asset, salvage value, and pattern of consumption.

+ Three commonly used types of depreciation are the straight line method, accelerated depreciation method, and units of activity method.

+ Remember to create a spreadsheet for your assets to keep track of depreciation, listing your items with date purchased and duration of your asset's useful life.

+ You do not have to use the same method of depreciation for your books and your taxes. Accelerated depreciation is the method you can use to accelerate depreciation in the first few years of your asset's life on your tax return, giving you more of a tax break in those first years. Thus you will have more cash flow to pay your equipment off earlier.

11

The Link Stands Alone, Part 2:
Liability Accounts in the General Journal

We are now on our way to nearing the end of explaining what accounting is. As I explained in the previous chapter, standalone links are special transactions that are unique to each business, miscellaneous in nature, and go through the general journal. Since these special situations are unique to your business, that means your accounting process involves a unique set of transactions. These transactions are also simpler to process because they are not part of a cycle, since only one portion of the LINKS figure is used. If you already guessed this, your grasp of the language of accounting is finally coming into light. I have finished describing all the assets in the chart of accounts, so now I will begin educating you on the liabilities that are part of the standalone—the general journal link. Figure 11-1 on the following page shows the general journal link with the liability accounts we will be covering in this chapter. My focus in this chapter is on the liabilities that most often occur in an everyday business. There are others, but the main ones here—inventory purchases receiving, customer deposits, payroll, sales tax payable, and notes payable—comprise the majority of liabilities small businesses encounter in business operations.

Figure 11-1

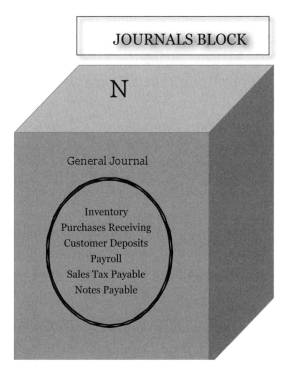

Holding Accounts

Inventory Purchases Receiving

The first account in the standalone link is inventory purchases receiving. This account was touched on briefly in chapter 7. It also has some association to the inventory account but not directly at first. For you to truly understand this account, you must recognize that it is strictly like a holding account that keeps prepaid amounts for inventory in it and is reduced when the inventory actually reaches the company. In other words, this is the holding account for product payments that have not yet been delivered to the company. This is all the account is, so it should be closely watched and reconciled periodically. The example touched on within chapter 3 in the inventory section shows the proper accounting method for these transactions. Sometimes, however, the purchase order for inventory for which a company is prepaying is not fully received when initially prepaying. There is a good method to use to help determine how much of an order has been received by setting up a type of spreadsheet to document these receipts. Say the company still has not received some of the items on purchase order #25. A great way to manage this account is by setting up a spreadsheet like the example in Figure 11-2.

Figure 11-2

Vendor M	
PO #25	$100,000
Invoice #23565	$(50,000)
Balance Vendor M	$50,000

Listing the vendor name, purchase order (initial order total) and invoice receipt will give the company a clear idea of what their pending purchase orders are, as well as balances pending with the vendors they order with. This spreadsheet can then be reconciled with the actual inventory purchases receiving account.

In summary, inventory purchases receiving is a prepaid liability account showing all prepayments (debits to the account) for inventory that has not yet been received and reductions (credits to the account) for the inventory that has been received.

Customer Deposits

In conjunction with inventory purchases receiving, customer deposits are also a prepayment account, although this account is associated with accounts receivable. As we discussed in chapter 7, customer deposits are considered a holding account. This holding account acts as a self-check to the many customers who deposit money for an order they placed. Most often, the customers make deposits since they have not yet received the product they ordered. As a result, the account is a liability to the company that is providing the product to the customer. A liability exists in this case from the goods not actually on hand at the company or its warehouse. Until the company receives the goods and the order is paid and shipped to the customer, the customer deposit liability will be present.

Payroll

If your company has employees, you will need to perform payroll accounting. Payroll is simple to set up when a computerized method is used. However, when a computerized method is not used, it can be somewhat tedious. Simply stated, payroll requires a few things to be set up properly. First, there should be a payroll payable account set up for each of the owners. This account will, as the year progresses, provide a running total of the payroll you are getting compensated for and will establish an easy breakdown for the tax return when done. Second, unemployment insurance and payroll tax expenses (for Social Security and FICA taxes) should be set up in the expenses section of the income statement in order to account for these deductions. In addition, there could be more deductions based upon the state your company is in (for state tax or child support, etc.). A typical way to journal your payroll is shown in Figure 11-3 on the following page.

Figure 11-3

1000 Cash	Credit
1000 Cash	Credit
1000 Cash	Credit
6091 Insurance, Employee Medical	Debit
6120 Payroll—Employee A	Debit
6121 Payroll—Employee B	Debit
6125 Payroll Tax	Debit
6163 Professional Fees—Payroll Service	Debit

This is a simple example and the process can become much more complicated depending upon what taxes or benefits are to be deducted from the employee's salary or wages. The best option is to set up everything up in a payroll software program and allow it to calculate all the deductions automatically.

Some practical information about wages is that for every employee, there is a wage base. A wage base is the amount of wages that are subject to Social Security taxes. Once the employee reaches that wage base during that year, the employee will no longer be subject to Social Security taxes. Therefore, the employee will continue to get Medicare and FICA taxes deducted, but Social Security is left out. Once a new year arrives, however, the employee will start having Social Security taxes deducted once again until the employee reaches the wage base in that year.

If your company is small and you do not have any employees, you can choose to do your payroll in a simpler way. It will still follow IRS rules in regards to paying taxes, but it will allow you a little more flexibility in reporting your payroll as the owner. Note that this is only an acceptable method for companies who are set up as a regular corporation or LLC. A general rule is that owners should not give themselves more than 35 or 40 percent of the predicted company profits, so this should be determined before you decide how much you are going to pay yourselves. Next, the proper tax should be paid in monthly deposits to the IRS for 941 taxes. This money will become a withholding amount for both Social Security and Medicare (employee and employer portions) and federal withholding.

Sales Tax Payable

Sales tax payable is present in any company that pays excise taxes. Generally speaking, any retail establishment that sells goods will be required by state law (unless your state does not have a sales tax for goods) to charge sales taxes to customers and pay sales taxes for the goods it sells. Furthermore, whenever an item is sold, there is a corresponding sales tax payable charge that should be allocated to that sale. As a result, a running total of sales tax payable will be present on the liabilities section of the balance sheet. Once the state excise taxes are paid (which are based on the amount of sales the company made for that time period), the sales tax payable account will be reduced by the amount of sales tax attributed to those sales and thus will zero out the account.

Notes Payable

Sometimes companies need to have a line of credit so they can have some extra cash in their business for large purchases they need to make. To secure a line of credit, you can go to your bank or investor to secure the line of credit. Based upon your company's credit, you are then able to borrow up to a certain amount of money. Typically a promissory note (a note specifying the line of credit, terms of the note, and when the note is required to be paid off) is issued to the company. In these next two journal entries, Investor B has *pledged* some money ($150,000) to provide a promissory note to the company (see Figure 11-4 below). The company will be required to pay back this loan, but since it will be considered a long-term obligation, it will have more time in which to do so. The investor can offer a certain amount of money for the company in the line of credit. Once the company reaches that amount, the company can no longer borrow money from that investor until it pays the line of credit down.

Figure 11-4

Date: 7/1/XXXX		
	Debit	**Credit**
Cash	$150,000	
Note Payable (Line of Credit)		$150,000
Memo: Company A Issued a Promissory Note to Investor B For Up to $250,000		

Date: 7/1/XXXX		
	Debit	**Credit**
Note Payable (Line of Credit)	$5,000	
Cash		$5,000
Memo: Draw On Line of Credit for Company Purchases		

As seen in Figure 11-4, there is an initial note payable, or line of credit. The investor will allow the company to borrow up to $250,000. When the company needs some cash to draw for company purchases, they will notify the investor, receive the cash—in this case $150,000—and credit it against the line of credit account. When payments are made to pay off the line of credit, the corresponding journal entry for line of credit debit and cash credit will be made. In addition, there should be an account set up to record the interest on the line of credit. For this to be properly accounted for, an interest payable account will be set up and entries recorded in the manner shown in Figure 11-5.

Figure 11-5

Date: 7/1/XXXX		
	Debit	**Credit**
Interest Expense	$200	
Interest Payable		$200
Memo: To Record July Interest on Investor B Line of Credit		

As long as all these accounts are set up with the proper memos, the trail of interest, payments toward interest, and line of credit will be accounted for and easily traced to each specific loan relating to it. Truthfully, a lot of transactions are involved in the process of loans and notes. However, if you remember to simply put the specific loan number or letter and month of interest, this will make the understanding of these complex accounts run much smoother. (Remember in chapter 4 when I gave you the tips about memos in your journal entries? This is where memos are crucial to understanding what your loan balances are and which loans you owe to whom).

Although this chapter has been short, I would like you to recognize that it gives you a great perspective of the liability accounts that are valuable parts of your accounting system.

You must be aware of these accounts and how they relate to your individual business. Proper recording of your liabilities is crucial in knowing how much you are holding on your books of credit, as well as how much you owe for your taxes. Classifying liabilities correctly will help you make the right decisions when determining how much of a product you may want to purchase or how many employees your company can afford to hire. Essentially, if you know what these liabilities mean and you handle them properly, you can keep your business's bottom line out of the red.

Chapter Eleven:
What's the Point?

Some standalone LINKS are considered liabilities.

+ These are special liability transactions unique to each business, miscellaneous in nature, and go through the general journal.

+ The focus in this chapter is on the liabilities that occur most often in everyday business, which include inventory purchases receiving, customer deposits, sales tax payable, payroll, and notes payable.

Holding accounts are special types of liability accounts.

‹ *Inventory purchases receiving* is a holding account that keeps prepaid amounts for inventory in it and is reduced when inventory actually reaches the company. The account must be monitored closely and reconciled periodically.

‹ *Customer deposits* is also a holding account that holds customers' deposits for orders they place. Most often, customers make deposits since they have not yet received the product they ordered.

Payroll is important for your staff if your company has employees, but even if you don't, it's important for you.

+ Payroll is simple to set up when a computerized method is used but is rather tedious and subject to errors when a computerized method is not used.

+ Guidelines for setting up your payroll require creating a payroll payable account for the owners. In addition, unemployment insurance and payroll tax expenses must be properly set up as well.

+ Deductions and taxes vary per state and employee.
+ Remember there are wage-base limits for employees. Once these employees meet the annual limit, they no longer have any Social Security taxes deducted from their gross pay.
+ Owners can pay themselves a salary based on their predicted company profits.

Sales tax payable is always due for a business selling merchandise.

+ Generally speaking, any retail establishment that sells goods is required by law to charge sales tax to customers, as well as pay sales tax for the goods it sells, unless the state does not have a state sales tax in place.
+ Whenever goods are sold, there is a corresponding sales tax payable charge that should be allocated to that sale.

Notes payable is your line of credit.

+ Based on your company credit, you can borrow up to a certain amount from a bank, subject to interest charges.
+ The note must be paid off within the term of the note.

12

The Link Stands Alone, Part 3:
Owners' Equity in the General Journal

In this chapter, I will touch on the capital investments owners make, the equity account that covers various owners' transactions, and retained earnings. To start off, we will highlight some definitions of these accounts, then go more in-depth with a typical transaction scenario. Knowledge of this information is highly important since it represents a company's solvency or insolvency.

Due to the complex nature of this account, my discussion will only touch on the basics, providing some general information for you to follow. As a small-business owner, you may or may not need to go beyond what we discuss here. If your company requires a more technical understanding of this subject, please refer to another source. A good reference book on this subject is *Barron's Accounting Handbook*. It provides definitions as well as examples for different scenarios in capital, owners' equity, and retained earnings.

Figure 12-1

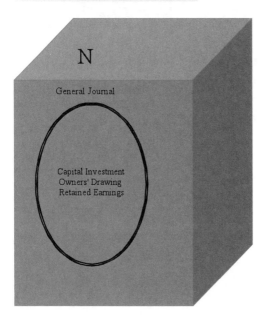

Invested Capital Account

There are a few types of owners' equity. Let's discuss *invested* or *paid-in capital* first; this is the amount invested by the owners in the company's assets or cash. Consider this example of an owner's initial capital investment: Say you decide to start your own business, and you have $100,000 you would like to use to invest into the company. To record this on the books, you will just debit your cash and credit your capital account. Figure 12-2 on the following page shows how to record these investments in the books.

Figure 12-2

Date: 1/1/XXXX		
	Debit	Credit
Cash	$100,000	
Capital		$100,000
Memo: To Record Owner Investment of $100,000 into the Business		

Now, what if you have some office equipment that you purchased many years ago and you wish to use it in the business to get started? All you need to do to record this equipment in your financial records is to figure out what you actually paid for the item(s) when you purchased them, then record them on your books as a capital investment into the business (see Figure 12-3 below for an example). You will be depreciating the item(s) later, just like any of your other depreciable assets (refer back to chapter 10 if you need a depreciation refresher).

Figure 12-3

Date: 1/1/XXXX		
	Debit	Credit
Office Equipment	$15,000	
Capital		$15,000
Memo: To Record Investment of $15,000 of Property into the Business		

These journal entries show the cash and office equipment accounts debited in the two first entries due to the money and office equipment invested into the company.

Owners' Drawing Account

The other type of owners' equity is called the drawing account. The drawing account is of particular importance to the owner and related to a number of things:

+ Personal charges for specific things not related to the business
+ Draws of cash for personal use
+ Investments of cash into the business
+ A place to record payments for things that were business related but were purchased through personal funds
+ Allocation of power, rent, telephone, etc. when a business is set up in at a home

For personal charges of specific purchases not related to the business, the owners' drawing account should be broken out. The business should determine when the chart of accounts is set up what different categories of personal purchases are most likely to occur. In the chart of accounts example on page 22–23, I have defined a few of the most common categories that reflect this personal use.

+ Sample Owner's Drawing Accounts
+ 3200 Owners' Drawing
+ 3210 Contributions
+ 3220 Dental
+ 3230 Draw
+ 3240 Insurance—Medical
+ 3250 Medical
+ 3260 Prescriptions

Typically the accounts associated with personal use are draws. Draws are money drawn out of the company's business checking account to be used by the owner(s) for purposes not related to the business. These amounts are not tax deductible. However, insurance—medical, medical, and prescriptions accounts are all classified for personal use and *are* considered deductible. Figure 12-4 shows a journal entry to record a medical transaction.

Figure 12-4

Date: 6/1/XXXX		
	Debit	Credit
Owners' Drawing—Insurance Medical	$1,500	
Cash		$1,500
Memo: To Record Annual Medical Insurance Premium		

A drawing account is generally known as the place to put miscellaneous transactions. Many business owners are unaware that this account is available for recording business purchases out of personal funds. Therefore many businesses fail to account for all transactions that actually qualify to record. Here is an example for the type of transaction I just mentioned. Say, for instance, that Owner A decided to buy some office supplies at the store but had only his personal account to purchase them with. He bought $500 worth of supplies. The recording entry would be set up like Figure 12-5.

Figure 12-5

Date: 6/1/XXXX		
	Debit	Credit
Office Supplies	$500	
Owners Drawing		$500
Memo: Purchase of Office Supplies with Personal Funds		

It is as simple as this. The transaction does not affect cash in the business account since the purchase was not made through this account. However, the office supplies expense account is debited to record the purchase, and offset is made to the owners drawing account.

So what happens when the owner makes a contribution into the business to add cash to the company? The owners' drawing will be recognized in this transaction, as shown in Figure 12-6.

Figure 12-6

Date: 6/1/XXXX		
	Debit	Credit
Cash	$15,000	
Owners' Drawing— Contributions		$15,000
Memo: Contribution of Cash into Business		

A final use of the owners' drawing account is that a home-based business owner can use it to deduct utility expenses, mortgage, phone, and Internet expenses. The way this is done is rather simple as well. To determine the amounts that can be deducted, the business owner must first calculate the percentage of square feet in the room that the office takes up. If customers use the bathroom, the company can also use a percentage of its square feet. Once this percentage of the building is calculated, it will be used to calculate all living expenses related to the business. For example, if the percentage of the home that the office was used in for Owner B's company is 25 percent then she would base all bills on this percentage. If the power bill for the month was $150, then the business portion allocated to the business would be $37.50 ($150 x .25). Figure 12-7 shows the journal entry to record this.

Figure 12-7

Date: 2/1/XXXX		
	Debit	Credit
Utilities—Power and Electric	$37.50	
Owners' Drawing		$37.50
Memo: Power Bill for January XXXX		

As this example shows, the expense will be debited and accounted for in the income statement section. The owners' drawing account is credited to offset the debit.

Retained Earnings

Retained earnings entails the profits in a company that are not distributed to shareholders as dividends but are either reinvested or kept as a reserve to pay off debt or buy a capital asset. This is the portion of stockholders equity that is increased by net income and reduced by net losses. In other words, your income summary is always closed to retained earnings at the end of your fiscal/calendar year. What this means is that all your income (all the sales you have less the sales discounts and other costs associated with your sales) less all your operating expenses (remember, your operating expenses are your selling, general and administrative, and other income and expenses broken down into categories and subcategories) is your retained earnings figure (the difference of the two). This figure will be your beginning balance for the start of your next fiscal year and continue to increase or decrease every fiscal/calendar year based on the income less operating expenses. Furthermore, your sales and operating expenses will not carry forward into your new year. As a result, you will have different totals every year, which changes your retained earnings amount yearly. Figure 12-8 shows how this works.

Figure 12-8

Your company has net sales of $80,000 in Year 1. Your operating expenses for the year are $30,000. To calculate your retained earnings, you will do this journal entry:		
Date: 12/31/XXXX		
	Debit	Credit
Sales	$80,000	
Operating Expenses		$30,000
Retained Earnings		$50,000
Memo: Closing Revenue and Expenses to Retained Earnings Year XXXX		

Note that sales is debited and expenses credited, which is opposite of what these accounts are normally charged. This is because the accounts are being closed out for the fiscal or year end. Their balances are zero after this journal entry. Also, you see that the retained earnings account's balance now is $50,000, the difference of the sales and operating expenses.

For Year 2, the company's net sales were $120,000 and operating expenses were $70,000. Calculating the retained earnings for Year 2 is the same as Year 1 (see Figure 12-9 on the following page). Now, however, the retained earnings account balance has changed to $100,000, the calculation of closing the revenues and expense accounts for two years.

Figure 12-9

Date: 12/31/XXXX		
	Debit	Credit
Sales	$120,000	
Expenses		$70,000
Retained Earnings		$50,000
Memo: Closing Revenue and Expenses to Retained Earnings Year XXXX		

In this chapter, you have learned some basic concepts about capital investments, owners' equity, and retained earnings, as well as how these accounts are important parts of your accounting. I highlighted in the beginning of the chapter how these accounts help determine the solvency or insolvency of your company. The concepts I outlined were just the beginning of situations and scenarios that could arise out of these accounts. As I said earlier, if your company has other types of transactions related to capital, owners' equity, or retained earnings that were not discussed in this chapter, you should refer to a book that deals with this subject more in-depth. This book only stresses the main parts of accounting and what is most relevant to a small business. Now that I have finished discussing all the links, your knowledge of accounting should be coming together.

Chapter Twelve:
What's the Point?

Owners' equity is considered investments of cash, property, or equipment.

- Investment of cash into the business when you initially start your business is considered a capital investment, and you will credit the capital account and debit cash to record it.

- If you are using equipment or property in the business that you already purchased at an earlier date, you simply record the asset(s) at the price you paid for them, crediting your capital account and debiting your assets separately so they can be depreciated.

Owners' equity is the multipurpose account.

- This account is used for personal charges not related to the business, draws of cash for personal use, investments of cash into the business, recording business-related purchases that were bought from personal funds, and allocation of a percentage of your utilities when operating a business in your home.

- Owners' equity is also known as owners' drawing account, which is generally a place to record miscellaneous transactions.

Retained earnings serves as your revenue and expenses summary closing account.

- You always close your revenue and expenses at the end of your fiscal/calendar year. Subtracting revenue minus expenses gives you a difference. The difference between these two is the retained earnings number, which will transfer into the beginning of the next year.

+ In the years following, the balance in retained earnings increases or decreases based on each year's revenue and expenses difference.

13

Need I Say More:
Accounting Beyond the LINKS Approach

Throughout most of this book, I have covered the main building block, which includes links that connect together in your transaction processing cycles, as well as a standalone link to cover the rest. What significance, then, do the other building blocks have for the rest of accounting? What part do they play in supporting and finalizing your accounting records accurately?

I have given you basic information on the other building blocks in this book, which consist of the general ledger, balance sheet, and income statement—otherwise known in accounting terms as the financial statements. I did give some examples in chapter 5 in which I tied the transactions generated from source documents to the LINKS journals and showed how the transactions posted into the general ledger, balance sheet, and income statement from there—the final posting process. Accounting ends here in these financial statements. Once you have entered all your data from source documents into your T-accounts and posted it into the LINKS journals, the transactions are all then posted into the general ledger.

The general ledger serves as a great audit trail. In other words, any and all transactions with the memos included—done in a chronological order—can be viewed in the general ledger. This is especially handy if your company loses source document data, or if your computer accounting program crashes and loses data. As long as you have saved copies of your general ledger, you can go back and recreate transactions. Also, if the IRS is auditing your records, the best data for them to review is in your general ledger.

As I explained in chapter 3, your balance sheet and income statement include only ending balances of all accounts included in the general ledger at a certain point in time. These financial statements will be vital in looking at your accounts from a general perspective to examine how much you may be spending on certain expenses, or have accumulated in accounts payable, or what your cash account balance is, for example.

From the perspective of the building blocks mentioned in this book, this should confirm to you that your greatest challenge in understanding accounting lies only in the journals building block. The financial statements that are generated from these journals give you your final data after your information is recorded in your books.

Chapter Thirteen:
What's the Point?

The significance the other building blocks have for the rest of accounting can be quickly summarized.

+ Accounting ends in the financial statements. Once you enter all your source document data into your T-accounts and post it into the LINKS journals, the transactions are all posted into the general ledger.

+ The significance of the general ledger is that it serves as a great audit trail, as well as a backup if your company loses data or your computer crashes. Your balance sheet and income statement include only ending balances of all accounts in the general ledger at a certain point in time.

+ The financial statements serve as a vital tool in examining how much you are spending on certain expenses, or have accumulated in accounts payable, or what your cash account balance is, for example.

14

Don't Read 'Em and Weep:
How to Interpret Your Financial Statements with Ease

Now that you have seen how the foundation of accounting starts and develops through specific building blocks through steps, you have gained a new interpretation of how accounting works. You have also looked at all the special journals, know that they link together, understand that they are all shown in the general ledger in detail, and know what the different special journals accounts are that are included in them. Furthermore, I have taken you through the process of special circumstances for transactions and how to account for transactions in those situations. In addition, you are now aware of all of the accounts in the chart of accounts and what types of transactions will affect each individual one. This is the language of accounting.

To round out the language idea, I am giving you some basic tools to give you a clear picture of what the numbers mean when they have gone through the processes mentioned above and are finally all brought together in their respective balance sheet and income statement. To grasp all these things is a daunting task of clarity. However, with the way I have explained it, I believe you can now realize that accounting is not a foreign language. It definitely has its own language, but you can grasp it with the simple tools I have used in the book.

What Does the Balance Sheet Say?

Your first main financial statement is the balance sheet. As we have previously discussed, all the numbers for the assets, liabilities, and owners' equity come together on the balance sheet. The balance sheet is the report to look at for determining what all your assets—current and long-term—are worth. You can also determine how much debt you owe—both current and long-term—in the liabilities section of the balance sheet. Finally, you will see the owners' equity section of the balance sheet. This section, which is represented by assets minus liabilities, represents the owners' holdings in the company. In addition, the retained earnings portion of owners' equity is where you will close net income or loss to at the end of every year. Whatever the net income or loss is, this number will be transferred to retained earnings. Once it is transferred into this, the income statement balances will convene to zero for the next year. If there is a net loss, over time the retained earnings will become negative. This symbolizes a company that is possibly short on cash and in need of restructuring its debt and expenses.

Trouble in Bank Loans

Bank loans on the balance sheet tell a lot about whether you are having financial troubles or are in a state of financial distress based on what the loan numbers look like. One of the most important things to note is that if your bank loans are increasing substantially, then your financial stability could be at risk. The most important item in the current liabilities is the notes payable account. This generally represents bank loans but could also be loans from companies or individuals (as shown in the example in chapter 11 in the notes payable section). More permanent bank loans such as these could indicate that the company needs long-term capital stock. However, if the loans get paid off regularly, there is not a reason to worry too much. In addition, if the notes payable account is substantially smaller than cash, there is no concern there either. Finally, bank loans should be looked at over the year's end to determine if they are growing faster than sales or profit. If they are, this is a sign of financial weakness.

Lessons from the Income Statement

The income statement is tied into the balance sheet in the overall net income or net loss number, as explained in reading the balance sheet. However, there is more to reading an income statement. All the numbers that represent the income statement are significant for a variety of reasons. First, the total net sales will show how much you are actually selling in your company on an ongoing basis. Also, the cost of goods sold (or the *cost of sales*) is the cost of the goods you are selling. When you deduct the sales less the cost of goods sold, this is your margin—how much you are profiting from the goods you are selling. Finally, the expenses comprise the final portion of the income statement. The total expenses are what it costs you to keep the business operating and functioning as a business. A great way to see if your business expense operations and net sales are doing well is to do a couple of simple calculations. One is to divide sales by cost of goods sold. This will determine if your costs of goods are high enough to retain enough profit to keep the business running well. Each industry has an average. For example, a retail furniture business should have about a 40 percent average of net sales divided by cost of goods sold. Anything lower could mean you are not charging enough for your goods and thus profit will drop. In addition, you can divide your operating expenses by net sales. In this example, a good percentage is 35 percent. Going any higher will greatly reduce profit and will be a sign that your company is incurring too many expenses to keep the business running and must reduce some of the operating costs. Finally, as a simple way to see the overall status of your operations, you will deduct the sales less cost of goods sold less expenses. This gives you your net income or net loss.

A New Beginning

The journey through this book has been an attempt to recognize that accounting is more than just the numbers. I have started with the foundation, given you the building blocks, shown you the prep work, focused on the most important building block (journals), and detailed those journals through the LINKS approach, all in an effort to help you visualize this process. Accounting is not a foreign language; it is simply a matter of following a step-by-step process to create accurate, understandable financial information. I hope this book has given you more knowledge about what accounting is and how to understand it better. Maybe you are on your journey to finally do your own accounting for your business.

Accounting, a foreign language? Not anymore!

Chapter Thirteen:
What's the Point?

The balance sheet says plenty about your business.

+ The balance sheets serves as a report to see what all your assets and liabilities—both current and long-term—are worth and how much you owe.

+ Owners' equity is also a part of the balance sheet, which is assets minus liabilities. This account represents the owners' holdings in a company.

+ The retained earnings portion of owners' equity is always your fiscal- or calendar-year sales minus company expenses.

+ When your company's bank loans are increasing substantially, your financial stability could be at risk. Bank loans should be looked at over the years to determine if they are growing faster than sales or profit. If they are, then it is a sign of financial weakness.

Many lessons can be learned from the income statement.

+ Net sales shows how much you are actually selling in your company on an ongoing basis.

+ The cost of goods sold is the cost of the goods you are selling.

+ When you deduct sales less cost of goods sold, this is your margin—how much you are profiting from the goods you are selling.

+ Remember, your operating expenses come in three category groups: selling, general and administrative, and other income and expenses. The total expenses are what it costs you to keep you operating and functioning as a business.

✦ Some simple calculations can help you determine if your operating costs are too high or not. Divide sales by cost of goods sold to help determine if your cost of goods is high enough to retain enough profit to keep the business running well. Another calculation is to divide operating expenses by net sales. This percentage should be lower than 40 percent for a furniture business, for example. Any higher and the operating expenses should get reduced. Finally, sales less cost of goods sold less expenses gives you your net income or net loss—your final net worth amount.

Index

Term definitions are found on page numbers in **bold**. Figures are denoted by *f* after the page numbers.

About the Author

Jeanine Pfeiffer, a graduate from Washington State University in Pullman, Washington, has a bachelor of arts in business administration with an option in accounting. She has twenty years of experience in accounting, and she has assisted many clients in a variety of industries including retail, distribution, manufacturing, service, professional service, and nonprofit. She has worked with large corporations, including Rena Ware International and Microsoft Corporation, as well as numerous small to mid-size companies. Her expertise includes many years helping small businesses restructure their accounting records by accurately identifying financial errors, updating financial data properly, and maintaining accurate financial data in a technologically efficient way. In her spare time, she likes to run and spend quality time with her family. Jeanine is CEO of Pfeiffers Accounting and Consulting, LLC and resides in Washington with her husband and three children.